"Through his many books, Jerry Bridges has been shepherding my soul since I first became a Christian sixteen years ago. He has done it again. As I have come to expect, he has provided a sea of theological matter in a drop of devotional language. Here you will find God-centered doctrine that is delectably deep and down to earth at the same time. I promise that if you read this book carefully and prayerfully, you will gain both an informed mind and an enlarged heart."

> —TULLIAN TCHIVIDJIAN, Pastor, New City Church,
> Fort Lauderdale, Florida; author, *Unfashionable:*
> *Making a Difference in this World by Being Different*

"Jerry Bridges and Bob Bevington have provided another marvelous instrument for guiding believers to the provisions of a gospel-blessed and gospel-driven life. In this volume the surpassing righteousness of Christ joined with the power of the Holy Spirit is clearly displayed from God's Word. Thanks from all of us who desire to make disciples that will follow Christ purposefully and passionately."

> —HARRY L. REEDER III, Senior Pastor,
> Briarwood Presbyterian Church, Birmingham, Alabama

"Forgiveness of sin and power to change—I can think of no more essential topics for a Christian to study than these twin blessings of the gospel. And I can think of no one better to write on these topics than Jerry Bridges. Jerry has provided for me over the years a constant diet of gospel-saturated writing, and here is a fresh feast. I trust you will enjoy it as much as I have."

> —C. J. MAHANEY, Sovereign Grace Ministries

"Jerry Bridges and Bob Bevington look at the Christian life through a wide-angle lens, examining the framework that supports, stabilizes and secures the believer's life in Christ. They teach elements of a distinctly biblical worldview, leaning upon the righteousness of Christ on one hand and upon the power of the Holy Spirit on the other. A wise and powerful book, one I heartily recommend."

> —TIM CHALLIES, author, *The Discipline of Spiritual Discernment*

"Thinking you understand the gospel but applying it only to salvation is like barely releasing your sail and slogging through the waves. *Bookends* will equip you to release that sail, catch the mighty wind of God, and see every 'book' in your life transformed."

—DEE BRESTIN, author, *Falling in Love with Jesus*

"With their latest publication, the authors display how sound theology is transformational and how understanding enhances true piety and produces profound worship."

—ROBERT M. NORRIS, Pastor, Fourth Presbyterian Church, Bethesda, Maryland

"Martin Luther said, 'Man in his search for truth is like a drunken peasant. You help him up on one side of his horse and he falls over the other side.' This book, perhaps more than any other, is designed to keep you on the horse living in the truth of the gospel. There are few books you will find more valuable on your shelf."

—JOE COFFEY, Lead Pastor, Hudson Community Chapel, Hudson, Ohio

THE BOOKENDS OF THE
CHRISTIAN LIFE

THE

BOOKENDS

OF THE

CHRISTIAN LIFE

JERRY BRIDGES
& BOB BEVINGTON

CROSSWAY BOOKS
WHEATON, ILLINOIS

The Bookends of the Christian Life

Copyright © 2009 by Jerry Bridges and Bob Bevington

Published by Crossway Books
   a publishing ministry of Good News Publishers
   1300 Crescent Street
   Wheaton, Illinois 60187

Cover design: The DesignWorks Group, www.thedesignworksgroup.com

First printing 2009

Printed in the United States of America

Unless otherwise indicated, Scripture quotations are from the ESV® Bible (*The Holy Bible, English Standard Version®*), © 2001 by Crossway Bibles, a publishing ministry of Good News Publishers. Used by permission. All rights reserved.

Scripture quotations marked KJV are from the *King James Version* of the Bible.

Scripture quotations marked NASB are from *The New American Standard Bible*, © The Lockman Foundation 1960, 1962, 1963, 1968, 1971, 1972, 1973, 1975, 1977, 1995. Used by permission.

All emphases in Scripture quotations have been added by the authors.

PDF ISBN: 978-1-4335-0551-5

Mobipocket ISBN: 978-1-4335-0552-2

Library of Congress Cataloging-in-Publication Data
Bridges, Jerry.
   The bookends of the Christian life / Jerry Bridges and
Bob Bevington.
      p. cm.
   ISBN 978-1-4335-0319-1 (hc)
   1. Justification (Christian theology). 2. Sanctification—
Christianity. I. Bevington, Bob, 1956–   . II. Title
BT764.3.B75   2009
234'.7—dc22   2008038697

LB			18	17	16	15	14	13	12	11	10	09
14	13	12	11	10	9	8	7	6	5	4	3	2	1

To all who, like the two of us,
recognize the utter insufficiency of their own
righteousness and strength,
and thus are desperate for the gospel.
And to our Triune God—Father, Son, and Holy Spirit—
who provides us with an impeccable righteousness
and an indomitable strength
through our union with Christ.

Only in the LORD . . . are righteousness and strength.
ISAIAH 45:24

FOR INDIVIDUAL OR SMALL GROUP STUDY

We encourage you to visit:

www.TheBookendsBook.com

where you'll find a free downloadable study guide and other tools to help you get the most out of this book.

CONTENTS

PREFACE

Over the past several years, as the two of us have shared with each other what God is teaching us through his Word and our experiences, we've concluded there are two foundational truths that give stability to our Christian lives. We've chosen to use the illustration of bookends to teach these two truths.

The Bookends of the Christian Life is a collaborative effort. So in every instance, whether the teaching or illustration is from one or both of us, we've chosen to use the plural pronouns *we* or *us*.

We would like to acknowledge Greg Plitt, Chris Thifault, Steve Myers, and Joe Coffey for their valuable assistance with the early drafts and Greg Bryan for the diagram design. Thanks also to Allan Fisher, senior vice president for book publishing at Crossway, for his support of this project, and to Lydia Brownback and Thomas Womack for their outstanding editorial work. In addition, we're grateful for each and every member of the Crossway team.

Lastly, we would like to thank Mitch Gingrich for his excellence in providing the free study guide at www. TheBookendsBook.com.

Jerry Bridges
Bob Bevington

BOOKS AND BOOKENDS

Most of us have experienced the difficulty of putting books on a bookshelf without having a set of bookends to keep them in place. You know what happens. The books on the end tip over. Then the books next to those tumble over the ones already fallen. Inevitably some end up on the floor. At this point we do what we should have done in the first place. We set a couple of sturdy bookends in position to support and stabilize the books on the shelf.

Think of your life right now as a long bookshelf. The books on it represent all the things you do—both spiritual and temporal. There's a spiritual book for each activity of your Christian growth and service, perhaps with titles such as *Church Attendance*, *Bible Study*, *Daily Quiet Time*, *Sharing the Gospel*, or *Serving Others*. The temporal books might include *Job Performance*, *Educational Pursuits*, *Recreation and Leisure*, *Grocery Shopping*, *Driving the Car*, *Doing the Laundry*, *Mowing the Grass*, and *Paying the Bills*, to name a few. Our temporal books are intermingled with spiritual books on our bookshelf, since all our activities are to be informed and directed by the spiritual dimension, just as Paul indicated: "Whatever you do, do all to the glory of God" (1 Corinthians 10:31).

This bookshelf of your life is a very active place. In the course of each day, as you pull one book after another off the shelf, life can get complicated. And the more committed and conscientious you are, the more frustration you might feel trying to manage all your various books simultaneously.

Without adequate bookends, even if we succeed in getting all our books to remain upright, their stability is precarious at best. If we try removing even one book, we may jostle those next to it, disturb the delicate balance, and cause books to topple and fall. Sometimes a single tilted book can knock over every other volume on the shelf in a catastrophic "domino effect." You can see why two sturdy, reliable bookends can make all the difference.

On top of life's complexity with its demands in both the spiritual and temporal realms, we often add a sense of guilt—guilt for what we should do but don't and guilt for what we do but shouldn't. Regrettably, many Christians struggle with one or more persistent sin patterns, often called *besetting sins*. They produce a sense of deep, gnawing, demoralizing guilt, which tends to hinder us from pursuing godly change. In fact, contrary to popular thinking, guilt by itself rarely, if ever, motivates a person to change. By itself, it only discourages us.

However, when rightly handled, guilt is actually good

for us. It's like pain. Pain tells us something's wrong and alerts us to do something to address its root cause. Consider leprosy, a disease that causes the loss of the sensation of pain in the hands and feet so that its victims frequently injure themselves without realizing it. In a similar way, a person without a sense of guilt can continue on a destructive path of sin without being aware of it. Such was generally the case of the self-righteous Pharisees, the ones Jesus opposed so vehemently.[1] Truth be told, there's probably something of the Pharisee in all of us, but in some, numbness to guilt is the prevalent condition of their heart. And their resulting sense of self-righteousness is far more dangerous than a sense of guilt.

On the other hand, the guilt-laden person is painfully aware of his situation. He struggles with his persistent sins, but sooner or later he fails again. He just doesn't know what to do. He has been told to "try harder," but that hasn't worked either. So he continues a life of quiet desperation.

Both the self-righteous Pharisee in his smugness and the guilt-laden person in his desperation have one thing in common: their bookshelf of life has no bookends.

The solution for both is the same. When we become united to Christ by faith, God places a set of bookends on the bookshelf of our lives. One bookend is *the righteousness of Christ*; the other is *the power of the Holy Spirit*. Though they're provided by God, it's our responsibility to lean our books on them, relying on them to support, stabilize, and secure all our books—everything we do.

Why are these two gracious provisions from God the

bookends of the Christian life? And how do we lean our books on them? This book will answer those questions, and these:

- How can I overcome persistent guilt?
- How can I deal with the pressure to measure up?
- Where can I find the motivation to grow?
- How can I live the Christian life with my heart and not just my head?
- How can I be sure God loves and accepts me?
- Where do I draw the line between God's grace and my works?
- Where can I find the strength to change in an authentic and lasting way?

The answers start with the first bookend. So continue with us as we explore the meaning and application of the righteousness of Christ.

PART ONE

The First Bookend: The Righteousness of Christ

CHAPTER ONE

THE RIGHTEOUSNESS OF CHRIST

I am not ashamed of the gospel . . . for in it the righteousness of God is revealed.

ROMANS 1:16–17

What is the righteousness of Christ, and why do we need it as the first bookend? The word *righteous* in the Bible basically means perfect obedience; a righteous person is one who always does what is right. This statement assumes there's an external, objective standard of right and wrong. That standard is the universal moral will of God as given to us throughout the Bible. It's the law of God written on every human heart. It's the standard by which each person will ultimately be judged.[1]

Our problem is that we're *not* righteous. As the apostle Paul put it so bluntly, "None is righteous, no, not one. . . . No one does good, not even one" (Romans 3:10, 12). That's strong language. We may quickly protest that we're not so bad. After all, we don't steal, murder, or engage in sexual immorality. We usually obey our civil laws and treat each other decently. So how can Paul say we're not righteous?

We respond this way because we fail to realize how impossibly high God's standard actually is. When asked, "Which is the great commandment in the Law?" Jesus responded, "You shall love the Lord your God with *all your heart* and with *all your soul* and with *all your mind*. This is the great and first commandment. And a second is like it: You shall love your neighbor *as yourself*. On these two commandments depend all the Law and the Prophets (Matthew 22:36–40). None of us has even come close to fulfilling either of these two commandments. Yet Paul wrote, "For all who rely on works of the law are under a curse; for it is written, 'Cursed be everyone who does not abide by *all* things written in the Book of the Law, and do them'" (Galatians 3:10). "All" is absolute. It means exactly what it says; not most, but all.

If we applied this same standard in the academic world, scoring 99 percent on a final exam would mean failing the course. A term paper with a single misspelled word would earn an *F*. No school has a standard of grading this rigorous; if it did, no one would graduate. In fact, professors often grade "on a curve," meaning all grades are relative to the best score in the class, even if that score isn't perfect. We're so accustomed to this approach we tend to think God also grades on a curve. We look at the scandalous sins of society around us, and because we don't engage in them, we assume God is pleased with us. After all, we're better than "they" are.

But God doesn't grade on a curve. The effect of Galatians 3:10 is to put us all under God's curse. And while it's one thing to fail a course at the university, it's altogether something else to be eternally damned under the curse of God. The good news of the gospel, of course, is that those who have trusted in Jesus Christ as their Savior will not experience that curse. As Paul wrote just a few sentences later, "Christ redeemed us from the curse of the law by becoming a curse for us" (Galatians 3:13). Let this truth sink deeply into your heart and mind: apart from the saving work of Christ, every one of us still deserves God's curse every day of our lives.

We may not commit "scandalous" sins. But what about our pride, our selfishness, our impatience with others, our critical spirit, and all sorts of other sins we tolerate on a daily basis? Even on our best days, we still haven't loved God or our neighbor as we should.

So we have to agree with Paul. None of us is righteous, not even one.

We know we need a Savior, so we trust in Christ to redeem us from the curse of God's law. But though we believe we're saved as far as our eternal destiny is concerned, we may not be sure about our day-to-day standing with God. Many of us embrace a vague but very real notion that God's approval has to be earned by our conduct. We know we're saved by grace, but we believe God blesses us according to our level of personal obedience. Consequently, our confidence that we abide in God's favor ebbs and flows according to how we gauge our performance. And since we each sin every single day, this approach is ultimately discouraging and even devastating. This is exactly why we need the first bookend. The righteousness of Christ changes all this.

JESUS CHRIST THE RIGHTEOUS ONE

What exactly is the righteousness of Christ? And how will it give us a sense of assurance in our day-to-day relationship with God? To begin answering those questions, let's go to one of our favorite verses of Scripture:

> For our sake he made him to be sin who knew no sin, so that in him we might become the righteousness of God. (2 Corinthians 5:21)

The first thing we need to consider in this verse is the sinlessness—the perfect obedience—of Jesus as a man living among us for thirty-three years. The Scriptures consistently testify to this. All four of the major writers of the New Testament letters attest to the sinless, perfect obedience of Jesus throughout his life on earth. In addition to Paul's words that Jesus "knew no sin," we have the testimony of Peter, John, and the writer of Hebrews: "He committed no sin" (1 Peter 2:22); "In him there is no sin" (1 John 3:5); Jesus was in every respect "tempted as we are, yet without sin" (Hebrews 4:15).

One of the most powerful indications of the sinlessness of Jesus came from his own mouth. To a group of hostile Jews to whom he'd just said, "You are of your father the devil," Jesus dared to ask the question, "Which one of you convicts me of sin?" (John 8:44–46). He could ask this question because he knew the answer—he was sinless. Jesus could confidently say of the Father, "I *always* do the things that are pleasing to him" (John 8:29). Every moment of his life, from birth to death, Jesus perfectly obeyed the law of God, the same law that is applicable to all of us.

Christ's obedience was tested by temptation (Matthew 4:1–11; Hebrews 4:15), and the intensity of his temptation was greater than any we'll ever experience or even imagine. When we succumb to temptation, the pressure is relieved for awhile; but unlike us, Jesus never gave in.

As astounding as that is, it wasn't the epitome of Christ's obedience. The pinnacle of his obedience came when "he humbled himself by becoming obedient to the point of death, even death on a cross" (Philippians 2:8). *The obedient death of Christ is the very apex of the righteousness of Christ.*

Let's not miss the implications of this. At the cross, Jesus paid the penalty we should have paid, by enduring the wrath of God we should have endured. And this required him to do something unprecedented. It required him to provide the ultimate level of obedience—one that we'll never be asked to emulate. It required him to give up *his* relationship with the Father so that *we* could have one instead. The very thought of being torn away from the Father caused him to sweat great drops of blood (Luke 22:44). And at the crescendo of his obedience, he screamed, "My God, my God, why have you forsaken me?"

(Mark 15:34). The physical pain he endured was nothing compared to the agony of being separated from the Father. In all of history, Jesus is the only human being who was truly righteous in every way; and he was righteous in ways that are truly beyond our comprehension.

OUR SIN TRANSFERRED TO CHRIST

The second truth to note in 2 Corinthians 5:21 is that "for our sake he made him to be sin." This is Paul's way of saying God caused Jesus to bear our sin. Peter wrote something similar: "He himself bore our sins in his body on the tree" (1 Peter 2:24). So did the prophet Isaiah: "All we like sheep have gone astray; we have turned—every one—to his own way; and the LORD has laid on him the iniquity of us all" (Isaiah 53:6). Paul is telling us that God the Father took our sin and charged it to God the Son in such a way that Christ was made to be sin for our sake.

Now we can see what Paul meant in Galatians 3:13 when he said, "Christ redeemed us from the curse of the law by becoming a curse for us." He became a curse for us *because* he'd become sin for us. And by those words *for us*, Paul indicates that Christ did this in our place and as our substitute.

Imagine there's a moral ledger recording every event of your entire life—all your thoughts, words, actions, even your motives. You might think of it as a mixture of good and bad deeds, with hopefully more good than bad. The Scriptures, however, tell us that even our righteous deeds are unclean in the sight of God (Isaiah 64:6). So Jesus has a perfectly righteous moral ledger, and we have a completely sinful one. However, God took our sins and charged them to Christ, leaving us with a clean sheet.

The biblical word for this is *forgiveness*. In and of itself, forgiveness is a monumental blessing. Paul echoed David on this when he wrote, "Blessed are those whose lawless deeds are forgiven, and whose sins are covered; blessed is the man against whom the Lord will not count his sin" (Romans 4:7–8; Psalm 32:1–2). But how did God do this and yet remain perfectly holy and just?

He did it by causing the sinless Son to bear our sins, including everything that goes with them: our guilt, our condemnation, our punishment. That's what it took for God to wipe our moral ledger sheet perfectly clean and at the same time preserve his holiness and justice—the price had to be paid on our behalf; so the sentence was executed on our Substitute.

CHRIST'S RIGHTEOUSNESS CREDITED TO US

But it wasn't enough for us to have a clean, but empty, ledger sheet. God also credits us with the perfect righteousness of Christ "so that in him we might become the righteousness of God." This happens the same way Jesus was made to be sin—by transfer. Just as God *charged* our sin to Christ, so he *credits* the perfect obedience of Jesus to all who trust in him. In what is often called the Great Exchange, God exchanges our sin for Christ's righteousness. As a result, all who have trusted in Christ as Savior stand before God not with a clean-but-empty ledger, but one filled with the very righteousness of Christ!

The theological term for what we've just described is one of Paul's favorite words, *justification*. The word *justified* in Paul's usage means to be counted righteous by God. Even though in ourselves we're completely unrighteous, God counts us as righteous because he has appointed Christ to be our representative and substitute. Therefore when Christ lived a perfect life, in God's sight *we* lived a perfect life. When Christ died on the cross to pay for our sins, *we* died on the cross. All that Christ did in his sinless life and his sin-bearing death, he did as our representative, so that we receive the credit for it. It's in this representative union[2] with Christ that he presents us before the Father, "holy and blameless and above reproach" (Colossians 1:22).

There's an old play on the word *justified*: "just-as-if-I'd never sinned." But here's another way of saying it: "just-as-if-I'd always obeyed." Both are true. The first refers to the transfer of our moral debt to Christ so we're left with a "clean" ledger, just as if we'd never sinned. The second tells us our ledger is now filled with the perfect righteousness of Christ, so it's just as if we'd always obeyed. That's why we can come confidently into the very presence of God (Hebrews 4:16; 10:19) even though we're still sinners— saved sinners to be sure, but still practicing sinners every day in thought, word, deed, and motive.

The perfect righteousness of Christ, which is credited to us, is the first bookend of the Christian life. The news of this righteousness is the gospel. Christ's righteousness is given to us by God when we genuinely trust in Christ as our Savior. From that moment on, from God's point of view, the first bookend is permanently in place. We're justified; we're credited with his righteousness. Or to say it differently, we're clothed with his righteousness (Isaiah 61:10) so that as God looks at us in union with Christ, he always sees us to be as righteous as Christ himself.

And that changes everything.

THE PRESENT REALITY OF OUR JUSTIFICATION

From our point of view, however, we sometimes handle our books as though the bookend of Christ's righteousness is not in place on our bookshelf. We do this when we depend on our own performance, whether good or bad in our estimate, as the basis of God's approval or disapproval. And when we take this approach, our assurance that we stand before God as justified sinners inevitably fades.

How can we experience the righteousness of Christ as it was meant to apply to our daily lives? In Galatians 2:15–21, Paul provided much insight on this, beginning with this sentence:

> We know that a person is not justified by works of the law but through faith in Jesus Christ, so we . . . have believed in Christ Jesus, in order to be justified by faith in Christ and not by works of the law, because by works of the law no one will be justified. (Galatians 2:16)

In this single sentence Paul uses the word *justified* three times. The repetition emphasizes that we're justified not by our personal obedience to the law but by faith in Christ.

In this context, faith involves both *a renunciation* and *a reliance*. First, we must renounce any trust in our own performance as the basis of our acceptance before God. We trust in our own performance when we believe we've earned God's acceptance by our good works. But we also trust in our own performance when we believe we've lost God's acceptance by our bad works—by our sin. So we must renounce any consideration of either our bad works or our good works as the means of relating to God.

Second, we must place our reliance entirely on the perfect obedience and sin-bearing death of Christ as the sole basis of our standing before God—on our best days as well as our worst.

Just a few sentences later Paul wrote, "The life I now live in the flesh I live by faith in the Son of God, who loved me and gave himself for me" (Galatians 2:20). In the context of Galatians 2:15–21, it's clear Paul is still talking about justification, yet he's using the present tense. He writes of the life he lives *now* in the flesh. This raises an apparent problem. We know justification is a past event—the moment we genuinely trusted in Christ we were justified, declared righteous by God. That's why Paul wrote, "We *have been justified* [past tense] by faith" (Romans 5:1). So if justification was a point-in-time past event for Paul, why in Galatians 2:20 does he speak in the present tense: "The life I *now* live [today] . . . I live by faith in the Son of God"?

The answer to this question is important. It tells us

how to experience the application of the first bookend to our daily lives. For Paul, justification was not only a past event; it was also a daily, present reality. So every day of his life, by faith in Christ, Paul realized he stood righteous in the sight of God—he was counted righteous and accepted by God as righteous—because of the perfectly obedient life and death Christ provided for him. He stood solely on the rock-solid righteousness of Christ alone, which is our first bookend.

We must learn to live like the apostle Paul, looking every day outside ourselves to Christ and seeing ourselves standing before God clothed in his perfect righteousness. Every day we must re-acknowledge the fact that there's nothing we can do to make ourselves either more acceptable to God *or* less acceptable. Regardless of how much we grow in our Christian lives, we're accepted for Christ's sake or not accepted at all. It's this reliance on Christ alone, apart from any consideration of our good or bad deeds, that enables us to experience the daily reality of the first bookend, in which the believer finds peace and joy and comfort and gratitude.

Before battery-powered watches were invented, wristwatches had to be wound every day. A watch's stem was used not only to adjust the hands but also to wind up the mainspring. The gradual unwinding of the mainspring throughout the day drove the mechanism of the watch to keep time. The gospel of justification by faith in Christ is the mainspring of the Christian life. And like the mainspring in old watches, it must be wound every day. Because we have a natural tendency to look within ourselves for the basis of God's approval or disapproval, we must make a conscious daily effort to look outside ourselves to the righteousness of Christ, then to stand in the present reality of our justification. Only then will we experience the stability that the first bookend is meant to provide.

But if it's true God's acceptance of me and his blessing on my life is based entirely on the righteousness of Christ, what difference does it make how I live? Why should I make any effort? Why should I put myself through the pain of dealing with sin and seeking to grow in Christlike character if it doesn't affect my standing with God? We'll answer these questions in the next chapter.

CHAPTER TWO

THE MOTIVATION OF THE GOSPEL

For the love of Christ controls us.
2 CORINTHIANS 5:14

To explore the gospel's motivating power, we'll look at the experience of three Bible characters: a sinful woman who met Jesus, a highly respected Jew who encountered the holiness of God, and a self-righteous Pharisee who discovered he was dead wrong.

THE SINFUL WOMAN

One of the most profound examples of how the gospel motivates and transforms us is seen in the story in Luke 7:36–50 of a sinful woman who encountered Jesus. The story begins with a Pharisee named Simon inviting Jesus to his house for dinner. While Jesus and the other guests reclined at the table with their feet behind them in the manner of that time, a woman who was "a sinner" came with a flask of expensive ointment to anoint the feet of Jesus.

In those days, at a dinner for a special guest, it wasn't unusual for uninvited visitors to enter and sit around the edge of the room, listening to the table conversation. What made this incident remarkable was that a woman whose ill-repute was well known would dare to enter the house of a highly religious Pharisee.

But this woman did not come merely to hear the conversation. She was on a mission. Rather than take a seat at the edge of the room, she went straight to Jesus. As she stood at his feet, she began to weep—not just a few trickling tears, but so profusely that his feet became wet with them. Kneeling down, the woman loosened her long tresses—a shameful act according to the custom of the day—and began to dry Jesus' feet with her hair. Bending lower, she kissed his feet, then anointed them with the expensive ointment she had brought.

She hadn't preplanned her actions. Jesus was already at Simon's house when she "learned" (verse 37) he was there. She must have rushed home, grabbed the flask of expensive ointment, and hastened to the dinner. She wanted only to anoint his feet. The tears and the drying of his feet with her hair were spontaneous. The question naturally arises: why would she dare to do this? To answer, let's continue the story.

The woman's actions and the lack of offense from Jesus were duly noted by Simon, a self-righteous Pharisee. He concluded that Jesus couldn't possibly be a prophet, or else he would have known what sort of sinner she was and wouldn't have allowed her to touch him. Reading Simon's mind, Jesus told him a parable of a moneylender who had two debtors. One owed five hundred denarii, the other fifty. When they couldn't pay, the moneylender cancelled both debts. Jesus asked Simon, "Which of them will love him more?" Simon replied, "The one, I suppose, for whom he cancelled the larger debt." Jesus said, "You have judged rightly."

Jesus then compared the uncaring treatment he'd received from Simon to the woman's lavish acts of adoration. What prompted the difference? Jesus went right to the root: "He who is forgiven little, loves little." Since Simon sensed no need of forgiveness from Jesus, he showed little if any love for him.

By contrast, the sinful woman lavished her love on the Savior because she realized she'd been forgiven much. When was she forgiven? Though Luke doesn't tell us, the only way this story makes sense is to assume the woman had previously encountered Jesus and been forgiven for her sins at that time. She wasn't forgiven because she loved much; rather, she loved much because she'd been forgiven much.

We can trace three steps in the woman's experience. She'd become deeply convicted of her many sins through her initial encounter with Jesus. She then received from him the assurance that her sins were forgiven. These two steps—deep conviction of sin and assurance of forgiveness—prompted the third: love and gratitude on her part. The dinner at Simon's house provided an occasion for her to publicly display these feelings. She displayed much love because she'd been forgiven so much.

There's an important lesson here for all of us. Genuine love for Christ comes through (1) an ever-growing consciousness of our own sinfulness and unworthiness, coupled with (2) the assurance that our sins, however great, have been forgiven through his death on the cross. Only love that's founded on both of these foundations can be authentic and permanent. If we find we lack love for the Savior, one or both of these prerequisites are deficient.

You may be wondering why Jesus told the woman, "Your sins are forgiven," if he'd already forgiven them earlier. He wanted to make her forgiveness public. Remember, she was a well-known sinner with a bad reputation. Simon and his other guests needed to hear Jesus' words. And imagine what those words meant to the woman. She well knew what Simon and his guests thought of her. To be publicly reassured of her forgiveness must have sent her home with an even greater sense of love and gratitude for the Savior.

What about the ointment? Isn't sacrificial giving the point of the story? Yes and no. It's true the ointment was very expensive; it may have been worth nearly a year's wages. But don't miss the fact that her acts of worship included evidence of heartfelt gratitude and deep affection. The ointment was merely an outward symbol of a life now dedicated to Jesus. She was forgiven much, and she loved much; she gave not only her ointment but her heart as well.

When we've truly experienced the gospel, far from producing a "why bother to grow?" attitude, it has just the opposite effect. It motivates us to lay down our lives in humble and loving service out of gratitude for grace.

A HIGHLY RESPECTED JEW

Little is known about the prophet Isaiah except that he ministered in and around Jerusalem and had ready access to Judah's kings. As such, he was undoubtedly a highly respected and very moral man. Isaiah recorded the details of an encounter he had one day with God:

> I saw the Lord sitting upon a throne, high and lifted up; and the train of his robe filled the temple. Above him stood the seraphim. Each had six wings: with two he covered his face, and with two he covered his feet, and with two he flew. And one called to another and said: "Holy, holy, holy is the LORD of hosts; the whole earth is full of his glory!" And the foundations of the thresholds shook at the voice of him who called, and the house was filled with smoke. (Isaiah 6:1–4)

The threefold ascription by the angelic seraphim, "Holy, holy, holy," meant that they attributed an infinite degree of holiness to God. The entire scene, especially this revelation of God's holiness, had a devastating impact on Isaiah. Overwhelmed by acute awareness of his own sinfulness, he cried out in desperation, "Woe is me! For I am lost; for I am a man of unclean lips, and I dwell in the midst of a people of unclean lips; for my eyes have seen the King, the LORD of hosts!" (verse 5). This is remarkable considering Isaiah was a member of the religious elite, totally on the opposite end of the moral spectrum from the sinful woman of Luke 7. But righteous though he was in outward morality, in light of God's infinite holiness Isaiah essentially placed himself on the same plane as the woman.

As Isaiah anguished over his newly discovered sinfulness, God sent one of the seraphim with a burning coal from the altar. As he touched Isaiah's mouth with it, the seraph said, "Behold, this has touched your lips; your guilt is taken away, and your sin atoned for" (verse 7). In this good news, Isaiah heard the gospel. Like the sinful woman, Isaiah also experienced both the deep conviction of his sin and the assurance of God's gracious forgiveness. Isaiah's response was also similar. When he heard the voice of the Lord saying, "Whom shall I send, and who will go for us?" he responded, "Here am I! Send me" (verse 8). Isaiah gave his life in service to God. He essentially offered himself as a blank check, to be filled in as God saw fit.

Isaiah's experience parallels that of the sinful woman. Though we don't know exactly what brought about her deep consciousness of sin, it was undoubtedly connected with being in the presence of Jesus and sensing the vast gulf between his holiness and her sinfulness. With Isaiah we see the same three-step process: first, acute realization of one's own sinfulness in the light of God's holiness; second, hearing the gospel that one's sins are forgiven; and finally the response of gratitude, love, and surrender leading to action.

We may not think we are as sinful as the woman in

Luke 7; we're certainly no more righteous than Isaiah. But wherever we are on the moral spectrum, we all need to experience this same three-step process deep in our souls. For the sinful woman and Isaiah, these steps came suddenly and dramatically. For many of us, such realizations may come in stages as we gradually grow in the Christian life. But whether suddenly or slowly, we should aim to increase our awareness of God's holiness and our sinfulness, coupled with an ever-deepening understanding of the meaning and application of the gospel. As we do, we, too, will respond with genuine gratitude and commitment to God; we'll experience the motivating power of the gospel, and our lives will be progressively transformed.

THE SELF-RIGHTEOUS PHARISEE

The religious credentials of Saul of Tarsus (later to become the apostle Paul) were outstanding. In his own words, if anyone had reason to be confident in the flesh—in one's own outward righteousness—he had more. He was born into the right family, became a Pharisee, and was outwardly blameless concerning the law of God. In his misguided, white-hot zeal, he even persecuted the church, thinking he was defending the holiness of God (Philippians 3:4–6). But on the road to Damascus, Saul discovered he was dead wrong (Acts 9:1–9). He recognized that this Jesus, whose followers he was persecuting, was none other than the Son of God.

He also concluded he was wrong about his own righteousness. Later, in his testimony recorded in Philippians 3:7–14, he referred to his own righteousness as *loss* and *rubbish*. Why? In his own words: "In order that I may . . . be found in [Christ], not having a righteousness of my own that comes from the law, but that which comes through faith in Christ, the righteousness from God that depends on faith." Paul utterly renounced his own righteousness as a means of attaining a right standing with God; instead, he relied solely on the shed blood and righteousness of Christ.

Did this cause him to become lax in his desire and effort to live a life pleasing to God? Again, his own words:

> Not that I have already obtained this [that is, becoming completely like Christ] or am already perfect, but I press on to make it my own, because Christ Jesus has made me his own. Brothers, I do not consider that I have made it my own. But one thing I do: forgetting what lies behind and straining forward to what lies ahead, I press on toward the goal for the prize of the upward call of God in Christ Jesus. (Philippians 3:12–14)

Paul's resting in Christ's righteousness rather than his own did not cause him to slack off in his pursuit of Christlikeness. Rather, it motivated him to *press on* and *strain forward*. Now his zeal was motivated not by a desire to earn God's favor but by love and gratitude for the righteousness of Christ that was his by faith. This is the motivating power of the gospel.

A LIVING SACRIFICE

We've looked at three different people who, after life-changing experiences with the gospel, were highly motivated by gratitude and love to worship, obey, and serve God. How should their experiences affect us? Paul sums it up:

> I appeal to you therefore, brothers, by the mercies of God, to present your bodies as a living sacrifice, holy and acceptable to God, which is your spiritual worship. (Romans 12:1)

Paul's word "therefore" means "in view of what I've said." Paul has just spent eleven chapters of Romans teaching about the gospel—the need for it, the provision of it, and its results. So in this verse he appeals to us *to respond* to gospel mercy by presenting our bodies as a living sacrifice to God. The expression "living sacrifice" denotes the entirety of our lives offered continuously to God. All believers are to do what the sinful woman, Isaiah, and Paul himself did—respond to God's great gift to us as sinners with deep-seated gratitude and love in action.

For many of us, our initial encounter with the gospel when we first trusted Christ occurred many years ago and is now a distant memory. Furthermore, the book of Romans may now be overly familiar to us; it just doesn't generate the same excitement it surely generated among the Roman believers when it was first read in their churches. The Christian life may now be more of a duty than a joyous response to the gospel. Consequently we may not experience the motivating power of the gospel.

That's why we need to intentionally bathe our minds and hearts in the gospel every day. Remember, we need the gospel not only as a door into an initial saving relationship with Christ, but also as the first bookend to keep our daily lives from becoming a performance treadmill. As we rely on Christ's righteousness in this manner, far from leading to a license to sin, it actually motivates us to deal with the sin we see in our lives by presenting our bodies as living sacrifices to God.

CHAPTER THREE

GOSPEL ENEMY #1: SELF-RIGHTEOUSNESS

Being ignorant of the righteousness of God, and seeking to establish their own, they did not submit to God's righteousness. For Christ is the end of the law for righteousness to everyone who believes.

ROMANS 10:3–4

There are many times when we fail to lean the books of our lives—our spiritual and temporal activities—on the first bookend of Christ's righteousness and instead trust in our own righteousness. Our books may start tipping over whenever we look in the mirror and wonder, "How well am I doing at personal obedience?" When we respond by resting in the assurance that we're successful enough, we harbor self-righteousness, which is Gospel Enemy #1. And when we respond with anxiety over the inadequacy of our performance, we harbor persistent guilt, Gospel Enemy #2.

Self-righteousness is an ugly word. It's associated with

snobbery, conceit, and a holier-than-thou attitude. We find such behavior repulsive, and we should. Yet when we assess self-righteousness at this level, we're considering it merely in terms of human relationships. The self-righteousness we refer to in this book goes deeper; it's a self-righteousness *toward God*. It's as if we tell him, "I'm doing so well; surely I deserve your blessing. You owe it to me."

Most of us would not actually venture to say something as presumptuous as that to God. But we essentially make this very statement whenever we depend on our own performance to merit any or all of the following six "A"-mazing blessings of God:

- *Approval* by God—his favor;
- *Access* to his holy presence—his fellowship;
- *Acceptance* into his family—his community;
- *Admittance* into heaven—his eternal life;
- *Appropriation* of our daily provisions—his earthly sustenance;
- *Ability* to live the Christian life—his strength.

Striving to merit these blessings may seem innocuous enough, but such an approach to God is downright dangerous. Paul says this kind of self-righteousness actually *nullifies* God's grace: "I do not nullify the grace of God, for if righteousness were through the law, then Christ died for no purpose" (Galatians 2:21). What's being nullified here is our ability to experience God's grace—the assurance that, based on the gospel alone, we receive all the above-mentioned blessings rather than the curse we justly deserve for our sin. Grace changes everything—now and forever! Its cost to God was infinite; its value to us is incalculable. So the thought that we could somehow forfeit the experience of that grace should make us shudder.

Paul implies that we nullify grace whenever we're self-righteous toward God. Who needs the cross if we can justify ourselves before God and earn his blessings by obeying the law? Do you see how this approach treats Christ as if he died for no purpose? Self-righteousness is a gospel enemy because it disregards, devalues, and discredits the gospel provision of the righteousness of Christ—the sinless life he lived for us and the sin-bearing death he died for us. Self-righteousness turns grace on its head because it views the sinner as deserving God's blessings rather than as undeserving.

Paul's letter to the Galatians displays how vital it is that we understand this. After a brief greeting, he gets right to the point:

> I am astonished that you are so quickly deserting him who called you in the grace of Christ and are turning to a different gospel—not that there is another one, but there are some who trouble you and want to distort the gospel of Christ. But even if we or an angel from heaven should preach to you a gospel contrary to the one we preached to you, let him be accursed. (Galatians 1:6–8)

The next verse is essentially a carbon copy, deliberately restated for emphasis: "I say again: If anyone is preaching to you a gospel contrary to the one you received, let him be accursed." If you think this is strong language, Paul later states, "I wish those who unsettle you would emasculate themselves!" (Galatians 5:12). Not a pretty word picture.

But this is in the Bible for a good reason. The "different gospel" Paul referred to was a doctrine of self-righteousness—a man-centered, performance-based, legalistic approach to making oneself acceptable to God by following religious rules. It was anti-gospel, a dangerous doctrine of self-justification. No wonder Paul is so adamant. Yet this approach to God is as prevalent in our day as it was in Paul's.

Here's a classic example. Picture yourself stopping a hundred people in the mall to ask the proverbial question, "If you died today and God asked you why he should let you into his heaven, what would you say?" You already know the prevailing answers: "Because I'm a pretty good person." "My good deeds outweigh my bad deeds." "I'm better than most people." People readily acknowledge they've sinned. After all, "I'm only human; nobody's perfect; everyone makes mistakes." But look carefully. What is the *object* of their dependence? It's their own relative righteousness (goodness), not the absolute righteousness of Christ alone. All these people are spiritually self-righteous. They see Christ's righteousness as irrelevant, if they see it at all. And even though they may be comparatively "pretty good" people—they nullify grace.

We've been discussing nonbelievers, but a similar question may be asked of us: suppose you have an urgent prayer request and God were to ask, "Why should I answer your prayer?" How would you answer? Would you immediately begin adding up your recent merit and demerit points?

One of us recently had such an experience. On the heels of asking God to meet a specific need, the thought occurred, "Lord, haven't I been serving you day and night for weeks?" Then the words from an old hymn came to mind: "My hope is built on nothing less than Jesus' blood and righteousness." It became a moment to repent from self-righteousness. Similarly, when we're tempted to appeal to God by pointing out that we haven't committed a particular kind of sin lately, we must remember: there's no difference between trusting God for salvation and trusting him for answers to prayer; in both cases we're dependent on Christ's righteousness alone.

Many today are banking on the hope that a just God will consider their good deeds to have enough redeeming value to offset the guilt of their bad deeds. But people who think like this make two dangerous assumptions that are inconsistent with Scripture; they misjudge God's justice, and they misconstrue the value of their own righteousness.

Jesus addressed these individuals in "a parable to some who trusted in themselves that they were righteous." There he described a Pharisee and a tax collector praying in the temple (Luke 18:9–14). The Pharisee was a member of the religious elite. His dependence on his own righteousness is apparent: "God, I thank you that I am not like other men, extortioners, unjust, adulterers, or even like this tax collector. I fast twice a week; I give tithes of all that I get."

He assumed his standing before God was secure, based on his perceived superior obedience to the law compared to others. But instead of gaining God's approval by his wide spectrum of religious activities and moral performance, the Son of God revealed his spiritual condition: "Not justified!" The gospel did not benefit the Pharisee; for him it was not good news.

We have a friend who looked back on the days before he trusted in Christ's righteousness and remarked:

> I was like a modern-day Pharisee. I went to church each week and sat there thinking how much better I was than my family members who slept in. I believed God accepted me because my sins were small compared to those of my friends. But once I understood the righteousness of Christ provided in the gospel, I realized I had been no more than a "good" unbeliever. I called myself a Christian, and sat alongside others who truly placed their faith in Christ's sacrifice and righteousness, but at best I was a nominal Christian—a Christian by name only—not by genuine faith in the gospel.

Even longstanding believers can fall into a similar trap—not with regard to our salvation but with regard to our perception of our standing with God. Unless we're vigilant about this, we're unlikely to recognize the remnants of self-righteousness in our lives. At times our approach to God becomes like preparing a résumé for a job application—we carefully include all our accomplishments, anything that might present us in a good light and make us more acceptable. Gradually, before we know it, our Christian life consists of continually trying to update our spiritual résumé to remind God and others of what we've done and not done. But in reality, the whole of our résumé is either sin or filthy rags (Isaiah 64:6). So every time we approach God in prayer, worship, or any other spiritual discipline, we must see our résumé only as he sees it—overlaid by Christ's perfect résumé.

To do battle with Gospel Enemy #1, we must gain a practical understanding of how self-righteousness works in the lives of believers. There are two categories of self-righteous believers. The first is the self-disciplined moralistic believer who partially embraces the gospel but feels deserving of one or more of those six "A"-mazing blessings on the basis of his or her religious performance. There's a fine line between such a person and the moralistic *un*believer; they look so much alike, we may not be able to distinguish between the two.

For believers in this category, much of their everyday faith and confidence resides in certain aspects of their own performance—their lack of scandalous sins, regular church attendance, serving others, Scripture memorization, daily devotions, tithing, or their sacrificial giving of time, talents, and material goods. Their dependence does not rest *solely* on the two-part atoning work of Christ—his perfect obedience in their place and his perfect sacrificial death in their place. Instead, Christ's finished work of substitutionary atonement seems vaguely inadequate to them, as though it somehow lacked power and validity.

In holding this view, they unwittingly make a demeaning statement about the Son of God: "Christ's righteousness *alone* isn't enough to make me acceptable to God—he needs *my* help in order to completely justify me." When we put it this way, we would all agree this is prideful: God can't possibly get *all* the glory if an essential part of my acceptance depends on me. This approach falls short of the glory of God in a subtle yet significant way.

A quote from one of our favorite books provides insight for Christians who, in practice, live as if God's love for them ebbs and flows according to their actions:

> When we have our quiet times for the day, or when we have given a tithe, we are confident of God's love toward us. But when our days become crowded and personal devotions end up neglected, we start to avoid God, sensing that we are under his wrath and anger. We imagine that God is waiting for us to get ourselves together before we again enter his presence. Such thinking betrays our failure to grasp the security of our union [with Christ] and the depth of God's love and consequently disrupts our communion with him.
>
> Making God's love contingent on our action is a sad but common misunderstanding in the church. Remember, a believer's union is never in jeopardy. For God's love is an eternal love that had no beginning, that shall have no ending; that cannot be heightened by any act of ours; that cannot be lessened by anything in us. While our sense of communion with God may fluctuate, his love does not grow and diminish. The wrath of God against the sin of saints was completely exhausted on the cross.[1]

Do you sometimes feel as if God's love for you ebbs and flows, depending on whether you've had a good quiet time? Do you know you're saved by grace but live as if God's day-to-day blessings are bestowed in accordance with your performance? Are you beginning to have doubts about the degree of freedom you actually have from the influence of self-righteousness?

Below is our list of probing questions designed to help you gain clarity. As you meditate on them, be brutally honest, for much is at stake. When you analyze your Christian walk:

1) Do you tend to live by a list of dos and don'ts?
2) Is it difficult for you to respect those whose standards aren't as high as yours?
3) Do you assume that practicing spiritual disciplines should result in God's blessing?
4) Do you feel you're better than most other people?
5) Has it been a long time since you identified a sin and repented of it?
6) Do you resent it when others point out your "spiritual blind spots"?
7) Do you readily recognize the sins of others but not your own?
8) Do you have the sense that God owes you a good life?
9) Do you get angry when difficulties and suffering come into your life?
10) Do you seldom think of the cross?

If you found yourself answering *yes* to at least half these questions, it's likely you're living under a stronghold of self-righteousness toward God. You need to see this for what it really is—a hideous enemy disguised as a satisfying glory. It will let you down and leave you hanging. Its satisfaction is as short-lived as an ice cube in the blazing sun; its glory has all the appeal of a well-dressed corpse. And at the end of the day this fact remains: no amount of personal performance will ever gain the approval of a holy God.

There's a second category of self-righteous believers. They also partially embrace the gospel, but they constantly live under a sense of guilt due to an acute awareness that the expectations they set for themselves are considerably under-fulfilled. They're displeased with themselves and assume God is also displeased. Their attitude can be deceptive: outwardly it may look like humility. But persistent guilt is a child of self-righteousness toward God. It's the belief that we should find our source of righteousness *within ourselves*, though we're painfully aware of our shortfall, as if to say, "I can do better, and I should do better"— emphasis on *I*. Like moralistic believers, these also border on unbelief. Only God knows their heart and whether they truly place their faith in the righteousness of Christ.

Most believers, including the two of us, often vacillate between these two categories. One day we feel good about our performance, and we look to God with confidence, harboring a subtle, unspoken attitude that we've earned his favor and deserve his blessing. We imagine a scene where we approach God with our list of attributes and accomplishments. Just like the Pharisee, we compare ourselves to others in an attempt to feel "justified." Although we primarily depend on the righteousness of Christ, we like to think we've added some of our own merit for good measure. But this is an insult to the gospel of the cross; we treat it as though our personal performance can add to its immeasurable and all-sufficient merit.

The next day we catch ourselves falling to temptation. Suddenly we are downcast and inwardly assume there is no way God is going to bless us until we straighten up. Instead of depending on the first bookend, we anxiously wait for our books to tip over and drop to the floor. This, too, is an insult to the gospel. We call it Gospel Enemy #2 because it treats Christ's death as though it were inadequate. We succumb to it when we fail to rely on the fact that the righteousness of Christ is never even slightly changed or diminished by our sin. Christ's work in the gospel is a finished work; its result is permanent. Even on our worst days we're to stand in the present reality of our justification in him.

Regardless of which of these two categories we lean toward, all of us are inclined at times to handle our books in ways that disregard the first bookend. We would even go so far as to say *every* believer has a built-in tendency to do this on a regular basis. You may find that statement alarming, but isn't it true we feel better about ourselves and our relationship to God when we're obedient compared to when we're disobedient? We must continually battle these two gospel enemies, self-righteousness and persistent guilt. They represent a form of unbelief that may not send us to hell but will rob us of fruitfulness, joy, and the assurance that God is for us and not against us, both now and forevermore.

Both enemies surrender to the same God-given, strategic weapon—the righteousness of Christ, the first bookend. We'll show how to apply this in chapter 5. But before we do, let's take some time to get to know Gospel Enemy #2 in more detail.

CHAPTER FOUR

GOSPEL ENEMY #2: PERSISTENT GUILT

I do not nullify the grace of God, for if righteousness were through the law, then Christ died for no purpose.

GALATIANS 2:21

As we've seen, by depending on our own performance to merit God's approval and blessings, we spurn the support and security of the first bookend. If we successfully measure up to our standards, we harbor Gospel Enemy #1, self-righteousness. If we fall short, self-righteousness can give birth to Gospel Enemy #2, persistent guilt. In this case, our dependence is still on our own righteousness, though we're painfully aware of its inadequacy. We view Christ's obedient life and death for us as though it fell short of its intended purpose—removing *all* our guilt so that we bear none of it ourselves. Here, too, our ability to experience the joys of God's grace is nullified.

Living under a stronghold of guilt is a story that goes all the way back to the garden of Eden. When Adam and

Eve sinned, they knew they'd done something wrong even before coming into the presence of God. Why? They felt *guilty*. So they covered themselves and hid from God. Later, when confronted by God, they resorted to finger-pointing (Genesis 3:7–13). And ever since, throughout human history, awareness of guilt is awakened at a very early age. How does this happen?

The Bible tells us that God has supplied every person with a conscience. It's part and parcel of all human hearts:

> For when Gentiles, who do not have the law, by nature do what the law requires . . . they show that the work of the law is written on their hearts, while their conscience also bears witness. (Romans 2:14–15)

The conscience is our God-given inner voice, an internal witness that testifies to the level of our personal obedience using God's perfect law as a measuring stick. Its voice is heard in both our mind and our emotions. Sometimes it whispers; sometimes it shouts.

Our conscience serves two important purposes for our good, just as pain does for our body. First, it sends off warning signals when we're about to go astray. This should remind us to renew our dependence on God's enabling strength, the second bookend (as we'll explore later). Second, when we sin, our conscience declares us guilty. This should remind us to renew our dependence on the cure for our sin-sickness, the righteousness of Christ crucified, the first bookend.

Our conscience is a good thing. But at times it can make us extremely uncomfortable. It can exert such a powerful force that it becomes downright painful. No wonder humans have invented such a vast array of escape mechanisms—everything from the subtle misuse of entertainment such as TV, movies, sports, video games, and hobbies, to the abuse of mind-altering substances such as alcohol and drugs, or even the unwavering pursuit of career or good works. These serve to numb the pain of our conscience, or to artificially make us feel better about ourselves, or both. The same can be said of addictions and preoccupations of every kind. Escape mechanisms are sinful responses that sidestep the God-given purpose of our conscience. This can lead to big trouble because it compounds sin upon sin.

When neglected or misused, our conscience, like our body, can malfunction. It breaks down and fails when we habitually embrace lies and double standards (1 Timothy 4:2). It becomes dirty and dysfunctional when we stubbornly cling to impurity (Titus 1:15). And repeatedly rejecting the voice of our conscience can eventually result in the shipwreck of our faith (1 Timothy 1:19). Failure to respond to our conscience in a biblical way can lead to self-loathing, clinical depression, and even suicide.

As we've noted earlier, all believers often commit sin (1 John 1:8, 10). Therefore we regularly hear the voice of our conscience. But, take note: *The message of the cross is absent from the signals sent by our guilty conscience*; it knows only the law. So all we hear from it is bad news, not good news.

In fact, embracing the nagging voice of our conscience instead of silencing it with the gospel is exactly how Gospel Enemy #2, persistent guilt, gets a stranglehold on believers. You may be there right now. And the sound may be deafening.

For others, the voice of conscience drones on like background noise. It becomes so "normal" they become unaware of being in the grip of guilt, even though it's making them spiritually (and possibly physically) sick.

Whether the voice of your conscience is extremely loud or barely audible, remember that you don't have to be a scandalous sinner to suffer from persistent guilt. So we should ask and answer the following questions carefully and regularly in order to identify the influence of this gospel enemy:

1) Are you painfully preoccupied with a particular habitual sin?
2) Are you discouraged or depressed by your failure to measure up?
3) Do you frequently experience anxiety that something's about to go wrong?
4) Does it appear God can use others but not you?
5) Is there something in your past you just can't seem to get over?
6) Do you fear that your past will come back to haunt you?
7) Do your difficult circumstances seem like God's judgment for your sin?
8) Do you steer clear of intimate relationships or small-group discussions?

9) When you sin, do you get a vague sense that somehow there'll be a price to pay?
10) Do you seldom think of the cross?

Persistent guilt sometimes incapacitates a believer. Take the case of Mark (not his real name). People at his church described him as conscientious and humble. Yet he struggled with anxiety and discouragement. And he tended to disappear from church for weeks at a time. After several years of observing this pattern, his pastor finally got to the bottom of it. Mark, it turned out, binged on Internet pornography three or four times a year. Each time he would succumb to paralyzing guilt. He couldn't face his Christian brothers and sisters until he could first "fix himself" for a few weeks.

Guilt-ridden believers often become desperate enough to seek help. A troubled believer we know went to a professional counselor and was advised, "You must learn to forgive yourself." But there's not a shred of biblical support for this concept. The truth is, our sin is real—we *are* guilty, just like our conscience tells us. And we have no authority or basis for making a self-declaration of forgiveness.

Instead, we must go back to the first bookend. Only the life and death of Christ offers a legitimate path to freedom from a guilty conscience—legitimate because it was a real, lived-in-the-flesh, finished righteousness, applied to us forever. It was an obedience "to the point of death, even death on a cross" (Philippians 2:8), where "Christ . . . offered himself without blemish to God, [to] purify our conscience" (Hebrews 9:14). What makes it legitimate *for us* is that he did it in our place as our substitute. Christ transfers (imputes, credits) his perfect righteousness to every sinner who is "in him" by faith (2 Corinthians 5:21). Yes, it's amazing and undeserved. But, as we saw earlier, when the Bible says we're just-if-ied by faith in Christ (Galatians 2:16), it means it's just-as-if *we*—like Christ himself— always obeyed. From the moment we're united to Christ by faith in the gospel, in God's own eyes we're permanently clothed in the very righteousness of Christ.

But we may not always experience this. Our awareness of our permanent standing may grow dim when we sin by embracing other treasures and dependencies. It's then we must return to our Advocate with the Father, Jesus Christ *the righteous* (1 John 2:1), and stand in the present reality of our justification. With our dependence back on the first bookend, the weight of our guilt melts away and we feel lighter than air—not because of anything we do or don't do, but because of the infinite, infallible, interminable righteousness of Jesus Christ our Savior.

Whereas guilt is a curse, a healthy remembrance of our sin is a blessing. Guilt ignores the cross but remembering our sin should drive us *to* the cross. Paul never forgot his sin. He not only remembered it, but he also used it to display the gospel:

> Formerly I was a blasphemer, persecutor, and insolent opponent. But I received mercy . . . and the grace of our Lord overflowed for me with the faith and love that are in Christ

Jesus. The saying is trustworthy and deserving of full acceptance, that Christ Jesus came into the world to save sinners,
of whom I am the foremost. (1 Timothy 1:13-15)

Another example is John Newton, who never forgot
his depravity as a notorious slave trader. But instead of wal-
lowing in guilt, he took it to the cross and left it there. And
he wrote the most famous Christian hymn, the one that
begins, "Amazing grace / how sweet the sound! / that saved
a wretch like me." To the very end, Newton remembered
both his sin and the gospel. On his deathbed at age eighty-
two, he said, "My memory is nearly gone, but I remember
two things: that I am a great sinner and that Christ is a
great Savior."[1]

As authors, we acknowledge that we stand on the
shoulders of some of the giants of the Christian faith whose
works are just as relevant today as when they were written centuries ago. We have tremendous respect for their
insights into the gospel, insights which have stood the test
of time. One such author is a little-known seventeenth-
century Puritan, Thomas Wilcox, who wrote *Honey out of
the Rock*,[2] one of the most helpful essays we've found on
dealing with persistent guilt. We've updated into modern
language a series of Wilcox's instructions for dealing with
persistent guilt:

• *Shift your focus away from your sin and onto Christ*: don't persist
  in looking upon sin; look upon Christ instead, and don't
  look away from him for a moment. When we see our guilt,
  if we don't see Christ in the scene, away with it! In all our

storms of conscience, we must look at Christ exclusively and continually.

- *Shift your focus to Christ, our mediator.* If we're so discouraged we cannot pray, then we must see Christ praying for us (Romans 8:34), using his influence with the Father on our behalf. What better news could we ever want than to know Jesus Christ—the Son of God, co-creator of the Universe—is addressing the Father on our behalf?
- *Shift your focus to Christ crucified, risen, and ascended.* When guilt persists, remember where Jesus is and where he's been. He has been upon the cross, where he spoiled all that can ruin us. He's now upon the throne of heaven, as our advocate and mediator. His state in glory doesn't make him neglectful or scornful of the guilty sinners he died to redeem. He has the same heart now in heaven as he had upon the cross.
- *Shift your focus to the glory of Christ.* If guilt still persists, remember that he pardons for his own name's sake (Isaiah 43:25; Ezekiel 36:22; 1 John 2:12), because in pardoning us he'll make us living monuments of the glory of the grace he purchased. It's Christ's own happiness to pardon, so he does. By embracing this truth, even the most desperate sinner's conscience can rest absolutely assured.
- *Shift your focus off of self-condemnation.* When our conscience relentlessly condemns us, remember that Christ will have the last word. He is judge of the living and the dead (1 Peter 4:5) and only he can pronounce the final sentence. Christ is the judge—not us or our conscience. So never for a moment dare to take the judge's place by proclaiming irreparable guilt when he proclaims hope, grace, and pardon. If we think our sin is too great to be pardoned, remember that Christ doesn't agree.
- *Shift your focus off of self-contempt.* If we're focused on hating ourselves, realize that we're focused on ourselves and not

on him. Self-contempt is a subtle form of self-centeredness, which is the opposite of Christ-centeredness. Unless
our self-contempt makes us look more at the righteousness
of Christ and the cross of Christ and less at ourselves, the
whole endeavor leads to death. Let our sin break our hearts
but not our hope in the gospel.

There's only one way to escape the grip of guilt: we
must flee to the gospel. It's the only perfectly safe and sufficient place to turn. Be assured, there's no lack of grace for
us there. John Owen, another of our favorite giants of the
faith, pointed to "the *infiniteness of grace*" and asked, "What
is our *finite guilt* before it?"[3] Owen knew we can never
exhaust the supply of the grace purchased by Christ's obedient life and sacrifice for us.

Here's one last consideration from our adaptation of
Honey out of the Rock, one that explains how our desper-
ate need for the first bookend results in our treasuring
Christ:

The greatness of Christ's merit is known best by sinners in
deep distress. The thirstier a man is, the more he'll prize a
cup of water; the more our sins break and burden us, the
more we'll treasure our Healer and Deliverer.

Join us in letting this quote resonate deeply within
you. Don't avoid the voice of your conscience; instead
deliberately and regularly remember your past sin and
acknowledge your present sin. Then return to the cross,
the epicenter of the unfathomable greatness of Christ's
merit. Don't be reluctant to feel thirst; it points you to

living water where you can cherish every drop of it he gives for what it really is—precious beyond comparison. And when those old guilt pangs stab at you, thank them for doing you a great service by reminding you afresh that there's a Deliverer who has already delivered you, a Healer whose stripes have already healed you (Colossians 1:13–14; Isaiah 53:5). And because of this, Christ is your all-surpassing treasure.

Not only do we recognize that we deserve none of this, but also we *love* the fact that we don't deserve it. It's a fact that displays and magnifies his grace. We share something in common with the sinful woman in Luke 7: our tears and our "ointment" don't earn a thing; they simply express our gratitude for the overwhelming way Christ has loved us in the gospel. We've been forgiven much, freed from much, and blessed much. So we love him much (but not nearly as much as he deserves). We continue to sin every day in ways that, if not big and scandalous, are nevertheless offensive and grieve his heart. And amazingly, he continues to love us, and keep us, and treasure us as the apple of his eye (Zechariah 2:8).

In the parable of the Pharisee and the tax collector in Luke 18:9–14, the tax collector took a far different approach from the self-righteous Pharisee. Trembling because of his guilt, he stood far off, eyes to the ground. He beat his breast and acknowledged his sinfulness. And he begged for God's mercy. Remarkably, Jesus declared him justified! And as if that good news were not astonishing enough, there's more. Jesus declared that in the future this tax collector would be *exalted!* And for what? Begging for mercy? Yes! Because his begging was a heartfelt acknowledgment of his sinfulness in the light of God's holiness; it was a burning expression of his desperate need of mercy—the very thing the gospel provides. His begging did not nullify the grace of God but exalted it.

If you're embracing persistent guilt, lay it down at Christ's feet and beg for a cleansed conscience—for the mercy, freedom, and peace he provides in his righteousness. That's the first step. In the next chapter we'll discuss more steps, important strategies for leaning our books on this first bookend.

CHAPTER FIVE

LEANING ON THE FIRST BOOKEND

"The Son of Man came to seek and to save the lost."

LUKE 19:10

On an actual bookshelf, once a bookend is set in place, it tends to stay put. The same is true with our spiritual bookends. God has set the first bookend of Christ's righteousness on the bookshelf of every true believer. It's infinitely solid and weighty. It's more secure than anything in the world. It will never pass away. And amazingly, it's ours to lean our books on.

But here's the rub: we're constantly inclined to disregard it and lean our books on our own righteousness instead of Christ's.

By "leaning" we mean *dependence*. Our culture frowns on the idea of dependence, but when it comes to the bookends of the Christian life, dependence is not only good, it's essential. The question becomes, "What is the *object* of our dependence; what are we dependent on?"

Dependence on the first bookend means relying on, trusting in, and placing our confidence, faith, and hope in the righteousness of Christ. Instead, we often attempt to lean our books on something that can't support their weight—the filthy rags of our own righteousness (Isaiah 64:6). When this happens, we must recognize it and shift our dependence back onto the first bookend. Otherwise, our books will fall.

In this chapter, we offer three focal points for dependence-shifting: (1) seeing ourselves as desperately lost sinners; (2) seeing the righteousness of Christ as all-sufficient for us daily; and (3) seeing and rejecting our functional saviors. Each involves *seeing* a vital aspect of our dependence on the gospel, seeing with "the eyes of your heart" (Ephesians 1:18). Such seeing touches our emotions, motivations, and decisionmaking. The seeing we're talking about is so deep that it shifts our dependence. When we see how extravagantly and undeservedly loved we are in the gospel, we see how much God is to be trusted and depended on.

The story of Zacchaeus (Luke 19:1–10) will help us frame the three focal points. He was a chief tax collector and a very rich man. Everyone knew how he got so wealthy; he blatantly bilked the common people out of their money. And yet he was drawn irresistibly when Jesus came to town. He was so short he had to climb a tree in order to see Jesus pass by, and then he hurried down when Jesus called him. Zacchaeus joyfully received him, and that day Jesus declared him saved.

Zacchaeus wasted little time demonstrating radical change. He called Jesus "Lord." And he immediately gave half his net worth to the poor and provided a fourfold restitution to everyone he'd ever cheated. But what if, over time, the gospel message of grace was to become distant and faint in his thoughts? Remembering the public approval he had gained from his generous repayments, Zacchaeus might be tempted (like every believer) to shift his dependence to his own righteousness. If this were to happen, what could Zacchaeus do to shift his dependence back? He could remember what he saw on that monumental day.

FOCAL POINT 1: SEEING OURSELVES AS DESPERATELY LOST SINNERS

As Jesus entered his home, Zacchaeus surveyed the crowd. They were grumbling. And as Jesus turned and faced them, about to explain the reason he would become the guest of such a conspicuous sinner, Zacchaeus felt their stares. The eyes of his heart opened, and he saw the depth of his depravity for the first time. "Oh no, *oh no!*—think of all the people I've cheated; think of all the people who are poor because of me!" Yet to his utter amazement and eternal joy Zacchaeus heard Jesus say, "The Son of Man came to seek and to save *the lost*."

Imagine Zacchaeus turning up his nose and saying, "Hey, who are you calling *lost*?" But Zacchaeus truly saw himself as a desperately lost sinner. Zacchaeus was just the kind of sinner Jesus was looking to save—a lost one.

Thomas Wilcox put it like this: "The gospel is for sinners, and only for sinners."[1] If you see yourself as a relatively good, moral, conscientious, church-going person, or one who's constantly being affirmed by others, you might wonder how you can possibly think of yourself as a lost sinner. But it should be obvious. When we step into the light of Christ's perfect righteousness, our utter depravity is exposed. Our righteousness is shown to be nothing more than filthy rags. Our supposed goodness is nowhere to be found. If you don't readily understand and humbly admit this, then genuinely ask God to open the eyes of your heart and expose your true depravity in light of his holiness. Reviewing the following list slowly and prayerfully may help:

- pride, selfishness, judgmentalism, lust, anxiety, greed;
- unthankfulness, unforgiveness, prayerlessness, covetousness;
- lack of self-control, insistence on having control;
- impatience, irritability, frustration, anger, resentment, jealousy, gossip, discontentment, bitterness, impure thoughts;
- failure to love God with all your heart, soul, mind, and strength;
- failure to love your neighbor as yourself;
- disregarding God, failure to trust God.

As God turns up the dimmer switch and pours more and more light on your life, you'll be shocked to see you're far more sinful than you ever dared to imagine. Remember, each and every sin is offensive to God. They demean his glory. Seeing just a single pattern of persistent sin in your life while simultaneously seeing the absolute holiness of God will cause you to cry out with Isaiah, "Woe is me! For I am lost" (Isaiah 6:5).

Our dependence shifts when the sight of our past sins and ongoing sinfulness grips our hearts in such a way that we become desperate for gospel grace—God's blessings in Christ toward those who deserve his curse. It shifts when we see our relative moral goodness for what it is— completely and totally inadequate before God. It shifts when we reject self-righteousness, when we renounce it and consider it rubbish (Philippians 3:8). It shifts when at the core of our being we see two large neon signs. The first one blinks: *Insufficient Righteousness*. The second sign never blinks; it simply reads *Undeserving*.

FOCAL POINT 2: SEEING THE RIGHTEOUSNESS OF CHRIST AS ALL-SUFFICIENT FOR US DAILY

Seeing the righteousness of Christ for what it is—all-sufficient—is a second strategy for shifting our dependence to the first bookend. Zacchaeus certainly saw it. Can't you hear him telling the story all over town? "I was a lost sinner, but I saw Jesus Christ the righteous; he came into our house, and so did salvation!"

As we've seen, there's a righteousness that *does* deserve God's blessing. It's a righteousness whose source is outside of us, not dependent on us. It's a real, historic, lived-in-the-flesh-to-the-very-end righteousness. It is Christ's righteousness. He never sinned *and* always obeyed—to the point of death, even death on a cross (Philippians 2:8).

But it's not enough to merely see the righteousness of Christ as all-sufficient; we must see it as all-sufficient *for us*. Jesus was perfectly obedient in *our* place, as *our* substitute. Have we lacked purity? Jesus was pure in our place. Have we lacked patience? Jesus was patient in our place. In every area where we see failure and sin, Jesus was successful at providing a perfect obedience that's credited to us.

Whenever we see Christ's righteousness as all-sufficient for us, shifting our dependence to it should be almost irresistible. But our hearts are deceitful (Jeremiah 17:9), and unless we're vigilant, our dependence eventually drifts back to us. We're inclined to hold up our best book from the bookshelf and think, "See this? This is good! I deserve God's blessing for this one!" In the words of the hymn, we're "prone to wander, Lord, I feel it." Staying dependent on the first bookend is a continual process, not a one-time event. We must actively work to see the righteousness of Christ as all-sufficient for us every day.

That is why each morning the two of us start our day by *preaching the gospel to ourselves*. We meditate on gospel promises by personalizing them in light of the sins we committed the previous day. We look at a different promise each day of the week. Since there are so many promises, we make substitutions from time to time. Here's an example of gospel promises. To personalize them, just fill in the blanks with your recent sins:

Every day: God, be merciful to *me*, the sinner! (Luke 18:13 NASB)

Sunday: But he was wounded for *my* transgressions of _____; he was crushed for *my* iniquities; upon him was the chastisement that brought *me* peace, and with his stripes *I* am healed. Like a sheep, *I* have gone astray; *I* have turned to my own way; and the Lord has laid on him *my* iniquity. (Isaiah 53:5–6)

Monday: He will again have compassion on *me*; he will tread *my* iniquities of _____ under foot. You will cast all *my* sins into the depths of the sea. (Micah 7:19)

Tuesday: Blessed am *I*, whose lawless deeds of _____ are forgiven, and *my* sins are covered; blessed am *I* against whom the Lord will not count *my* sin. (Romans 4:7–8)

Wednesday: There is therefore now no condemnation for _____ for *me*, as one who is in Christ Jesus. (Romans 8:1)

Thursday: And *I*, who was dead in *my* trespasses of _____ and the uncircumcision of *my* flesh, God made alive together with Christ, having forgiven *me* all *my* trespasses, by canceling the record of debt that stood against *me* with its legal demands. This he set aside, nailing it to the cross. (Colossians 2:13–14)

Friday: As far as the east is from the west, so far does he remove *my* transgressions of _____ from *me*. (Psalm 103:12)

Saturday: Though *my* sins of _____ are like scarlet, they shall be as white as snow; though they are red like crimson, they shall become like wool. (Isaiah 1:18)

Every day: Christ's work for *me* is finished! (John 19:30)

By preaching the gospel to ourselves every day, we regularly see ourselves as desperately lost sinners who have been rescued by the all-sufficient righteousness of Christ. This is a powerful force for shifting our dependence back onto the first bookend.

FOCAL POINT 3: SEEING AND REJECTING OUR FUNCTIONAL SAVIORS

It's possible for our dependence to reside on something other than either Christ's righteousness or our own. Sometimes we look to other things to satisfy and fulfill us—to "save" us. These "functional saviors" can be any object of dependence we embrace that isn't God. They become the source of our identity, security, and significance because we hold an idolatrous affection for them in our hearts. They preoccupy our minds and consume our time and our resources. They make us feel good and somehow even make us feel righteous. Whether we realize it or not, they control us, and we worship them.

Before Zacchaeus met Christ, money was his functional savior. He would do anything to get it. But the day he met Jesus, he clearly saw his functional savior as insufficient, and he rejected it with lightning-fast reflexes and heartfelt urgency. His was a forceful and dramatic shift in dependence.

Sadly, we're all prone to embrace functional saviors. Like Zacchaeus, we must identify and reject them. But it's not always easy. Our deceitful hearts clutch, cloak, and protect them. And functional saviors take many forms. For some, it takes the form of a self-destructive addiction. For others it could be something that otherwise would be good or harmless if they weren't dependent on it—activities or things. It could be television, family, friends, sleep, caffeine, partying, not partying, eating, not eating. It could be career, fashion, investment accounts, approval of others, material possessions, peer status, good looks, recreation, spectator sports, having a clean house, or working out at the gym. It could be just about anything, including moderate living, asceticism, philanthropic giving, or even ministry.

If you haven't already figured out what your functional saviors are, try filling in these blanks:[2]

I am preoccupied with _____.

If only _____, then I would be happy.

I get my sense of significance from _____.

I would protect and preserve _____ at any cost.

I fear losing _____.

The thing that gives me the greatest pleasure is _____.

When I lose _____ I get angry, resentful, frustrated, anxious, or depressed.

For me, life depends on _____.

The thing I value more than anything in the world is _____.

When I daydream, my mind goes to _____.

The best thing I can think of is _____.

The thing that makes me want to get out of bed in the morning is _____.

Through the prophet Jeremiah, God issued a strong warning against functional saviors, calling them broken cisterns:

> My people have changed their glory for that which does not
> profit. Be appalled, O heavens, at this; be shocked, be utterly
> desolate, declares the LORD, for my people have committed
> two evils: they have forsaken me, the fountain of living
> waters, and hewed out cisterns for themselves, broken cis-
> terns that can hold no water. (Jeremiah 2:11–13)

God's warning is abundantly clear. Functional saviors cannot be depended on. They leak. They leave us empty and thirsty. To depend on them requires us to forsake God. He declares this to be unprofitable, appalling, shocking, and evil. The flipside is that when we identify and remove our functional saviors, our dependence is free to shift to the true and living God, the fountain of living waters.

God, who sees the heart (Psalm 44:20–21), knows when his beloved adopted children fall prey to a functional savior. He sometimes mercifully intervenes. As a surgeon will skillfully remove a cancerous tumor before it kills, so our master physician will cut away our sinful attachments. We may experience this as a very painful process. But it's all at the hand of an all-wise God who has loved us to the point of his own excruciating death.

We've seen this in our own lives in the form of testing and trials—increasing physical disabilities, disappoint-ments in our work and careers, being defrauded in some business transaction, and even such mundane experiences as lost luggage at the baggage claim, to name a few. We also realize that in the end God will remove us from our bodies—our ultimate functional savior—through physi-cal death. Though dying may be painful, this too, when you really stop to think about it, is an act of incredible mercy.

THE THREE FOCAL POINTS ILLUSTRATED

Following is a real-life testimony of a very gifted pastor friend of ours.[3] Note how his dependence shifts away from self-righteousness and functional saviors. Note how seeing his own depravity and the all-sufficiency of the gospel provided leverage for his shift. What do you think will happen to his ministry as a result?

I've found it to be incredibly challenging to give up the belief system that has sustained me so long—one built on an initial forgiveness and then fed through a powerful combination of pride and fear. Pride that stemmed from the performance of spiritual disciplines. Pride that pointed to the obvious signs of success—we were, after all, named in the Fastest Growing 100 Churches in America. And most of all, pride that was fueled by the approval of others. But fear may have been an even greater motivator. Fear of being exposed as less than what people expect. Fear of not being as smart, as spiritual, or as competent as I should be. Fear of not measuring up. And fear of Luke 12:48—"To whom much was given . . . much will be required."

The belief system of a pastor is bound to come out in his preaching, at least in subtle ways. My emphasis was always on grace, but it was also laced with the discipline of effort and inner strength to be what God called us to be. The result was either pride or defeat. My preaching has changed as a result of the gospel going deeper inside me.

The truth is, I have existed as a pastor with gods in my closet. There were times when these gods sustained me.

And giving them up has caused more death this year than I would like to admit. The closet is still not empty. But the death of these gods has made me ravenous. Without the gospel as my source of security and significance, I would die. So as one who has vacillated between self-sufficiency and depression, gospel-driven transformation is both liberating and terrifying.

There are some in our church who have not yet redis-covered the gospel this way. There are others who hear the terrifying part but not the liberating part, and they sit on pins and needles. Many of them will leave soon, I think. But there are many others who have felt the shackles start to fall off and, like me, they're filled with an inexpressible and glorious joy.

Rediscovering the gospel is an ongoing process. Our church is a big ship to turn. I would never attempt to turn it if the approval of others was as vital to me as it was a year ago, and if I hadn't been changed by the Good News. This is a much better place to be—even if I'm rejected by some; even if attendance falls. As a sinner-pastor, I stand in *dependence* on grace to plant and water gospel seeds, recognizing that God himself gives the growth.

As you can see, the shifting of dependence is often a difficult, even painful pursuit. And it can be an ongoing battle. But when all is said and done, what could be better than leaning on a real God, with real and lasting righteous-ness, who saves, satisfies, fulfills, and sustains us now and forever?

As we move on to discuss the second bookend, we must never lose sight of the first, because every book must lean on both. Without the first bookend, the second would be useless, leading only to self-righteousness. Many Christians, including us, have made the mistake of glossing over the first bookend to get to the second, only to find frustration and despair. We pray that won't happen to you, and that you'll find it irresistible to lean on the first bookend while you learn to depend on the second—the power of the Holy Spirit.

PART TWO

The Second Bookend:
The Power of the
Holy Spirit

CHAPTER SIX

THE POWER OF THE HOLY SPIRIT

For God gave us a spirit not of fear but of power.
2 TIMOTHY 1:7

The ability of the gospel to motivate us as believers increases as our reliance on the first bookend grows. But motivation by itself is insufficient; we also need the strength to carry out our motivation. An athletic team playing a clearly superior opponent needs more than a desire to win. It also needs ability and power. The same is true in the Christian life. We're up against a triumvirate of powerful opponents: the world, the devil, and our own flesh. We don't have the strength within ourselves to engage these powerful foes. That's why God provided the second bookend, the power of the Holy Spirit, to enable us.

BE STRENGTHENED

Second Timothy was Paul's last letter, written just before his death. It was filled with words of exhortation to Timothy to encourage him to persevere in his God-given ministry in spite of increasing opposition. In that context Paul wrote, "You then, my child, be strengthened by the grace that is in Christ Jesus" (2 Timothy 2:1).

Grammatically, Paul's words "be strengthened" are in the form of what we may call "a passive imperative." The passive voice indicates something done *to* us, not by us, while the imperative is used to command someone to do something. When we want someone to do something, we ordinarily use the active voice, not the passive. For example, when Paul urged Timothy to "preach the word" (4:2), he used the active imperative. But Paul's words "be strengthened" indicate that something is to be done *to* Timothy. He's to be strengthened by something outside himself. That something is "the grace that is in Christ Jesus."

We usually associate grace with the first bookend, thinking of verses like Ephesians 2:8: "For by grace you have been saved through faith." But grace in the New Testament is actually much broader—it includes all the blessings God has given us through Christ. Those blessings can generally be classified under two categories: privileges and power.

The grace in 2 Timothy 2:1 is the blessing of power. It's the same category of grace we see in 2 Corinthians 12:9 as the Lord tells Paul, "My grace is sufficient for you, for my power is made perfect in weakness," and Paul responds, "Therefore I will boast all the more gladly of my weaknesses, so that the power of Christ may rest upon me." Here God equates his grace with his power; power that can be experienced only through human weakness. So when Paul wanted Timothy to be strengthened by the same divine power he had experienced, he urged Timothy to be strengthened by grace.

How is Timothy to respond to this command? By faith he's to rely on the power of the Holy Spirit instead of his own resolutions, self-effort, or willpower. He's to acknowledge that without Christ he can do nothing (John 15:5). Just as he must look outside himself to Christ's righteousness for his standing before God, he must also look outside himself to the power of the Holy Spirit for his strength to live the Christian life. And the same is true for us.

THE ROLE OF THE HOLY SPIRIT

This grace or power is "in Christ Jesus." God has deposited all the blessings he has for us "in Christ," because Christ's obedient life and death purchased every blessing God has for us. But if the power is in Christ, why are we calling it the Holy Spirit's power?

Although all of God's blessings are in Christ, they're distributed and applied to us by the Holy Spirit. Paul wrote, "You were washed, you were sanctified, you were justified in the name of the Lord Jesus Christ and *by* the Spirit of our God" (1 Corinthians 6:11; see also Ephesians 2:20–22; Romans 8:2–17). Though we could call the second bookend "the power of Christ," we've chosen here to emphasize the Holy Spirit's work in applying this power to our lives. John Owen explained:

> Everything God does he does as the triune God. Each Person of the Trinity is involved in every action of God. Yet at the same time each Person has a special role to fulfill in that work. . . . There is no good that we receive from God but it is brought to us and wrought in us by the Holy Spirit. Nor is there in us any good towards God, any faith, love, obedience to his will, but what we are enabled to do so by the Holy Spirit.[1]

Paul's prayer for the Ephesians provides insight into the dynamics of how the three members of the Trinity concurrently work through the ministry of the Holy Spirit:

> I bow my knees before the Father . . . [asking] that according to the riches of his glory he may grant you to be strengthened with power through his Spirit in your inner being, so that Christ may dwell in your hearts through faith. (Ephesians 3:14–17)

Here Paul appealed to the Father, asking him to grant the Spirit to provide strengthening power so the Son would indwell the Ephesian believers.

We also emphasize the Holy Spirit's role because we believe it's often misunderstood and undervalued in Christian circles today. In many instances when the work of the Spirit is recognized, the focus is limited to his gifts for ministry rather than his role in transforming our lives. But the truth is, the Spirit's role is essential in our day-to-day sanctification: "And we all, with unveiled face, beholding the glory of the Lord, are being transformed into the same image from one degree of glory to another. For *this comes from the Lord who is the Spirit*" (2 Corinthians 3:18). Apart from the transforming power that comes from "the Lord who is the Spirit," our faces remain veiled, we don't see God's glory, and we aren't transformed.

Now that we have clarified the role of the Holy Spirit, you might ask, "What's our role?" It is the same as it was with the first bookend—faith. Here, however, it's the action of leaning our books on the second bookend. And as we've already observed, faith involves both *renunciation* and *reliance*. We have to first renounce all confidence in our own power and then rely entirely on the power of the Holy Spirit. We must be enabled, not merely helped. What's the difference? The word *help* implies we have some ability but not enough; we need someone else to supplement our partially adequate ability. By contrast, *enablement* implies that we have no ability whatsoever. We're entirely powerless. We can do nothing. But when by faith we renounce self-sufficiency and embrace reliance on the power of the Holy Spirit, we receive divine empowerment, enablement, and strength for personal transformation and ministry.

THE SOVEREIGNTY OF THE HOLY SPIRIT

However, we must always remember that the Holy Spirit is sovereign in his work. Our renunciation and reliance do not tie him to any rules or course of action. He's not a genie we summon into action by rubbing the magic lamp of our prayers. Sometimes when we're tempted he allows us to twist in the wind, so to speak—he doesn't come to our rescue immediately. Why? So that we might learn afresh that without his enabling power we can neither fight sin nor grow in character nor minister effectively. At times like these he uses our weakness and even our sin to drive us back to the first bookend for the assurance that the sins that now seem so shameful in our eyes are truly forgiven and that we still stand before God clothed in the righteousness of Christ.

At other times we're amazed as we experience the tremendous power of the Holy Spirit enabling us to resist the temptation of some persistent sin pattern, or making us clearly effective in some occasion of ministry where we've been keenly conscious of our own weakness and inability. In these times, without the Spirit's sovereign work divinely enabling our minds, hearts, and actions, we would be given over to the whims of the flesh and the frailties and feebleness of our humanity.

Both of us have experienced these two extremes on many occasions and can testify to the fact that the Holy Spirit truly is sovereign; he works according to his will, not ours. But whether he temporarily withholds or dramatically manifests his power, we may be sure he's working in every instance according to his own plan and timetable to accomplish his goals for our lives.

THE SPIRIT'S SYNERGISTIC WORK

At this point we need to understand in greater depth how the Holy Spirit works in the believer's life. The Bible teaches that the Spirit applies his power to our lives in two different ways. The first we call his *synergistic* work, which refers to occasions that combine our effort with his enabling power. But this isn't a pure synergism, as if we and the Spirit each contributed equal power to the task. Rather, we work as he enables us to work, so we use the expression *qualified synergism.*

We're 100 percent dependent on his power in order to participate in the work, as the psalmist illustrated: "Unless the LORD builds the house, those who build it labor in vain. Unless the LORD watches over the city, the watchman stays awake in vain" (Psalm 127:1). Two activities are mentioned: building a house and watching over a city. The Lord's involvement isn't one of helping but of building the house and watching over the city. At the same time, the builder builds and the watchman watches. The verse's message is that the Lord doesn't merely help the builder and the watchman; he's totally involved with them in this qualified synergism. He supplies all the enabling power, and they do all the tangible work.

There are many such examples in the New Testament. We're to "put to death the deeds of the body" —the sin that remains in us—yet we do so "by the Spirit" (Romans 8:13). We're to use the spiritual gifts we've received to serve God and other people, yet we do so "by the strength that God supplies" (1 Peter 4:10–11).

Perhaps we see this qualified synergism most clearly in Philippians 2:12–13: "Work out your own salvation with fear and trembling, for it is God who works in you, both to will and to work for his good pleasure." In this sentence, Paul refers to *work* three times. *We* are to work—to apply ourselves with utmost seriousness and vigilance. But we're to do so with the recognition that God provides us with both the motivation (the will) and the power (the work) to obey.

Toward the end of this letter, after describing how he'd learned to be content in any and every circumstance, Paul summed up the concept of qualified synergism with a sweeping, dramatic statement: "I can do all things through him who strengthens me" (Philippians 4:11–13). We're fully and wholeheartedly engaged in the work as the Spirit's enabling power works in us.

THE SPIRIT'S MONERGISTIC WORK

The second way the Spirit applies his power to our lives is his *monergistic* work, in which he works *alone* in us and for us but completely independent from us. The monergistic work of the Holy Spirit begins when he gives us new life by causing us to be born again (John 3:5–6; Titus 3:5–6). This is a mysterious process, one we cannot understand or control: "The wind blows where it wishes, and you hear its sound, but you do not know where it comes from or where it goes. So it is with everyone who is born of the Spirit" (John 3:8).

Through the new birth, the Spirit gives us the gifts of repentance and faith (Acts 11:18; Ephesians 2:8). He inclines our hearts to obey God: "I will put my Spirit within you, and cause you to walk in my statutes and be careful to obey my rules" (Ezekiel 36:27). Prior to the Spirit indwelling us, our hearts were bent only toward sin; we couldn't please God no matter what we did or didn't do (Romans 3:10–12; 8:7–8). The supernatural work of the Holy Spirit alone creates this new desire in us; it happens apart from any willpower or decision-making processes of our own.

The Spirit also gives us a unique type of assurance of our salvation. Paul wrote, "The Spirit himself bears witness with our spirit that we are children of God" (Romans 8:16). How the Holy Spirit interacts with our spirit to bear witness that we're God's children is a mystery we cannot comprehend, but we experience its reality applied to us quite independently from any effort on our part to feel like a child of God.

The sixteenth-century *Heidelberg Catechism*, which unfortunately is little known among believers today, provides a framework for understanding the monergistic work of the Spirit. It's structured around three words: *guilt*, *grace*, and *gratitude*. These words refer to *our* guilt, *God's* grace, and *our* response of gratitude. We saw this threefold sequence earlier as we looked at the experiences of the sinful woman, the prophet Isaiah, and the apostle Paul. But how do we come to recognize our guilt and to understand and believe the gospel so as to experience God's grace? It's by the monergistic work of the Spirit (John 16:8; 2 Corinthians 4:4, 6). Thus, our resulting heartfelt gratitude to God for his grace is also vitally connected with the monergistic work of the Holy Spirit.

Jesus often referred to the Spirit of God as our "Helper" (John 14:16, 26; 15:26; 16:7). This word may also be translated Encourager, Advocate, Intercessor, Counselor, or Comforter. John Owen often called him "the Spirit of consolation." Consolation is a vital, monergistic ministry of the Holy Spirit, yet we seldom recognize it. As we engage in spiritual warfare with the world, the devil, and our own flesh, we often experience discouragement because of our sin or difficult circumstances. At times like these, the Spirit may surprise us with his encouragement. Both of us have experienced this. It usually comes when we're keenly aware of how undeserving we are of such a reenergizing blessing.

Sometimes we're conscious of the monergistic work of the Holy Spirit and sometimes not. Either way, we can be confident that throughout our lives he's always at work to accomplish God's purpose both monergistically and synergistically.

THE SEAMLESS APPLICATION OF MONERGISM AND SYNERGISM

We must understand both ways the power of the Holy Spirit is applied to our lives so we can discern how to contribute effort, even though it is likely we won't fully know which one the Spirit is applying at any given time. The writer of Hebrews provides helpful insight:

> Now may the God of peace . . . equip you with everything good that you may do his will, working in us that which is pleasing in his sight, through Jesus Christ, to whom be glory forever and ever. Amen. (Hebrews 13:20–21)

The two prayer requests here seem redundant at first, but upon closer inspection, we see that they aren't. The first is that God will *equip* us with everything good we need to do his will. This is his synergistic work. Do we need understanding of God's will? He'll supply it. Do we need the power to perform it? He'll provide it. Do we need providential circumstances, materials, people, or other resources? He equips us. But the writer's second request is that God will *work in us* whatever is pleasing in his sight. This is his monergistic work. He performs it without our effort, and sometimes in spite of our effort.

Most of us are aware of spiritual needs in our lives. We prioritize areas of sin we need to put off and aspects of the Spirit's fruit we need to put on. We pray and ask God to enable us by his Spirit to change in those areas. That's our spiritual growth agenda. It's good to have such an agenda, and God is pleased to honor our requests and to enable us to change over time. But meanwhile the Holy Spirit has his own agenda, which works in conjunction with the agenda he has placed within our hearts.

So while the Holy Spirit is working in us synergistically to enable us to accomplish our growth agenda, he's at the same time working monergistically to change us according to his agenda. As we contemplate this, we can only bow in wonder and adoration at his sovereignty, grace, and power: his sovereignty that he does his work in us, his grace that he condescends to do so, and his power that he is both now and eternally uncontainable. We say with the psalmist, "Bless the LORD, O my soul, and all that is within me, bless his holy name!" (Psalm 103:1).

We hope you would now agree we're just as dependent on the second bookend as on the first. All our books—our spiritual and temporal activities—must be supported by *both* the righteousness of Christ and the power of the Holy Spirit, or they'll fall off the shelf of our Christian life.

There are three important similarities between these two bookends. Both are infinitely solid and weighty because they're provided by God Almighty. Both require faith, which includes a renunciation of our own resources and a reliance, or dependence, on God's. And both are blood-bought, life-changing fountains of grace—blessings beyond measure, such that he gets all the glory.

There are also important differences. The first bookend represents his work *for* us and *outside* of us. It's totally finished and complete. We can never become more righteous or less righteous in our standing before God once we're clothed with the perfect, completed righteousness of Christ. The second bookend represents his work not only for us but *in* us. This work, whether monergistic or synergistic, is always a process. It will never be finished and complete in this life.

There is another difference, one that is often misunderstood in ways that can have dire consequences. It involves our response to the bookends, the answers to questions such as, "What do I do? What's my responsibility? What part do I play?" Our response to the first bookend is always passive; our part is simply to receive it. The same is true with the monergistic work of the Holy Spirit in the second bookend. But the synergistic work of the Holy Spirit in the second bookend requires an active response from us; there is something we are responsible to do. It is vital we understand this distinction and how it works. So we devote the entire next chapter to explaining it.

CHAPTER SEVEN

DEPENDENT
RESPONSIBILITY

But if by the Spirit you put to death the deeds of the body,
you will live.

ROMANS 8:13

So where does our own responsibility come into the picture? In responding to the synergistic work of the Holy Spirit in the second bookend, where do we draw the line between what we are to do and what he is to do? Does such a line even exist?

Throughout the New Testament, the answers to these questions are consistent: we're both responsible *and* dependent. This is true whether we're referring to our growth in character or our effectiveness in ministry. In the same letter in which Paul urged Timothy to be "strengthened by the grace that is in Christ Jesus," he also exhorted him, "Do your best to present yourself to God as one approved, a worker who has no need to be ashamed" (2 Timothy 2:15). "Do your best" could also be translated

"Be diligent" or "Make every effort." Timothy's dependence on the Spirit did not negate his own responsibility to work hard.

Paul's life exemplified dependent responsibility. Referring to his ministry he wrote, "For this I toil, struggling with all his energy that he powerfully works within me" (Colossians 1:29). *Toil* means to labor to the point of exhaustion, and *struggling* translates a Greek word from which we get our English word "agonize." Obviously Paul was unusually gifted, and he worked extremely hard. He was a theologian, an evangelist, a church planter, and a cross-cultural missionary. Meanwhile he partially or completely supported himself through his trade of tent-making (Acts 18:3–4; 20:34–35). And yet Paul's giftedness wasn't a substitute for relying on the power of Christ as applied by the Holy Spirit. Paul realized he needed divine enablement to perform "with all his energy that he powerfully works within me."

Some have misunderstood Paul's words to mean he never got tired, as if Paul were a mere pipeline through which Christ's power flowed. Rather, the Spirit worked through Paul in such a way that all his physical, mental, and emotional faculties were fully engaged. The Spirit's role was not to make Paul's own energy unnecessary but, rather, to make it *effective*. And of course even Paul's natural abilities and spiritual giftedness were the result of the Spirit's work.

Although Colossians 1:29 is in the context of Paul's ministry, the same principle of dependent responsibility applies to our effort to grow in Christlikeness. In Colossians 3:12–14, Paul makes it clear we're to actively "put on" a number of Christlike character traits. Yet he elsewhere calls a similar list of traits "the fruit of the Spirit" (Galatians 5:22–23). So while the putting on is 100 percent our responsibility, we're at the same time 100 percent dependent on the Spirit of God to produce the fruit.

Earlier we looked briefly at Philippians 2:12–13, calling attention to our dependence on the Spirit of God for our transformation as seen in the phrase, "For it is God who works in you, both to will and to work." Here we want to emphasize Paul's preceding phrase: "Work out your own salvation with fear and trembling." We're to work diligently at our Christian growth but in the assurance that God is at work in us.

DILIGENT EFFORT

This theme of diligent effort runs throughout the New Testament, as in these examples:

- We're to watch and pray that we enter not into temptation (Matthew 26:41).
- We're to cleanse ourselves from every defilement of body and spirit (2 Corinthians 7:1).
- We're to discipline our body and keep it under control (1 Corinthians 9:27).
- We're to be steadfast, immovable, and always abounding in the work of the Lord (1 Corinthians 15:58).
- We're to train ourselves to be godly (1 Timothy 4:7).
- We're to strive for holiness (Hebrews 12:14).

- We're to make every effort to grow in Christian character (2 Peter 1:5–7).
- And we're to be diligent to be found by him without spot or blemish (2 Peter 3:14).

All these Scriptures are action statements. They express something we're to do. They're not merely good advice; they're moral commands. Here's another such command: "For this is the will of God, your sanctification: that you abstain from sexual immorality" (1 Thessalonians 4:3). When Paul indicated that "this is the will of God," we readily understand that he's expressing a moral imperative. Yet all of those action statements listed above could also be prefaced by the expression, "For this is the will of God."

This is serious business. These statements aren't merely commands of a human father or a teacher or coach. No, they're expressions of the will of *God*—the very God to whom each of us shall give account (Romans 14:12). Yet how often do we casually gloss over moral imperatives like these as we come across them in our Bible? We seldom stop to consider they're the direct commands of the infinitely holy God, the absolute sovereign of the universe.

Scriptures like these not only express the moral will of God, but they also reveal our responsibility. They require diligent effort and hard work. On the other hand, all our hard work is to be done in dependence on the Holy Spirit to enable us and to make our work effective. There's no conflict between our work and our dependence. In fact, the harder we work, the more absolute our dependence on the Spirit must become.

THE MEANS OF GRACE

As we look to the Spirit to work in us and enable us to work, we should realize that he uses various spiritual instruments, often called "the means of grace." They're the means by which we're "strengthened by the grace that is in Christ Jesus." So you can see why this next section should get our attention.

When we speak of someone using instruments, usually the object being worked on is passive. When the surgeon uses instruments to remove our appendix, we're completely passive. But this isn't true of the way the Holy Spirit uses his instruments. We have a responsibility to respond to each means of grace the Spirit provides. We're to participate in using them to our spiritual advantage. The term *spiritual disciplines* is used to describe this process and to emphasize our responsibility. Through practicing the spiritual disciplines, we avail ourselves of the means of grace.

As we practice these disciplines, it's of paramount importance that we keep two truths in mind. First, the disciplines themselves are not the source of spiritual power. Only the Holy Spirit is. The disciplines are his instruments to transmit his power. Second, the practice of the disciplines doesn't earn us favor with God or secure his blessings. Christ has already done that through his sinless life and sin-bearing death for us. That's why the grace we need to live the Christian life is "in Christ Jesus." It bears repeating: we must be on our guard to avoid seeing the practice of the disciplines as either the source of power we need or the meritorious cause of receiving the power.

Daily Communion with God

The first means of grace we will look at is the spiritual discipline often referred to as the *quiet time* but which might better be called *daily communion with God*. For many, the elements of this are a Bible reading plan and a prayer list. Both are important, but they're effective only to the extent that they facilitate the experience of fellowship with God. Instead of simply reading a chapter or two of the Bible, we need to reflect on and pray over what we read, asking him to reveal what he has for us in the Scriptures before us. Our reading becomes a conversation, a process of talking to God and listening to him. We may ask him questions as we seek a deeper meaning or a specific application of a given passage. We interact with a living Person. And in so doing, we experience communion with God. The psalmists longed to encounter God (Psalms 27:4; 42:1–2; 63:1–3; 73:25–26), and that should be our goal as we practice this spiritual discipline.

The other four means of grace that we'll consider are rooted in and become a part of this daily experience of fellowship with God.

The Gospel

Within the scope of our communion with God, the most important means of grace is the gospel. Once again we turn to 2 Corinthians 3:18: "And we all, with unveiled face, beholding the glory of the Lord, are being transformed into the same image from one degree of glory to another. For this comes from the Lord who is the Spirit."

Basically Paul was saying that it's through beholding the glory of the Lord that we're transformed more and more into his image. In what way do we behold his glory? We get the answer when we read this verse in context (2 Corinthians 3:8–4:6). It's the gospel that reveals Christ's glory. Therefore, to behold his glory we must gaze into the gospel by faith. As we do this, the Spirit will transform us more and more into his likeness.

As we have surveyed the writings of theologians and pastors as far back as the sixteenth century, we see this recurring theme: the gospel is the primary instrument of spiritual transformation.

If this is true, how should we respond? What spiritual discipline should we practice most diligently? We should bathe our hearts and minds in the gospel as part of our daily communion with God. To use an increasingly popular expression, we should "preach the gospel to ourselves every day." But since the gospel is only for sinners, we should begin each day by acknowledging that we continue to be practicing sinners—saved sinners to be sure, but still sinning every day in thought, word, deed, and motive. However, we're not to wallow in our sin. Instead we enter into communion with Christ at the foot of the cross where God forgave us our sin and canceled the record of debt that stood against us (Colossians 2:13–14).

Then the gospel will motivate us to want to live lives that are pleasing to God.

All of Scripture

Although the gospel is the focal point of the entire Bible and the most important means of grace, it's not the only one. Paul prayed for the Colossian believers that they might "be filled with the knowledge of his will in all spiritual wisdom and understanding, so as to walk in a manner worthy of the Lord, fully pleasing to him" (Colossians 1:9–10). How are we to know God's will? It's revealed to us in the Scriptures.

Earlier in this chapter we looked at some of the moral imperatives in the New Testament. These are only a sample. We need moral imperatives like these to show us what spiritual transformation looks like. And we need the promises of God's provision, protection, and power as they're found in the Scriptures to keep us going when times are tough.

We respond to this means of grace by consistently bringing our minds under the renewing and transforming influence of Scripture. Paul wrote, "Do not be conformed to this world, but be transformed by the renewal of your mind, that by testing you may discern what is the will of God, what is good and acceptable and perfect" (Romans 12:2). It's the Spirit who transforms us, but in this instance he does so through the renewing of our minds. And though the Scriptures aren't explicitly mentioned, they're clearly implied. There's no other way to renew our minds except through exposure to God's Word. We need to regularly listen to Bible-centered preaching, and we need to diligently pursue Bible study and Scripture memorization, all as a means of grace pointing us to communion with God.

Prayer

Prayer is another instrument the Holy Spirit uses as a means of grace to strengthen us. Whenever we pray, we're almost always expressing our dependence in one form or another. When we pray, we consciously acknowledge our helplessness and inability to accomplish by ourselves anything that's pleasing to God. Our response to this means of grace is obvious: we're to practice the spiritual discipline of prayer by regularly asking him to work in us and enable us to work. This includes daily periods of extensive prayer as well as brief, spontaneous prayers when we're in the heat of the battle.

Here again we must keep in mind that the Spirit of God is sovereign over when and how he works through the instrument of prayer. He certainly hears our requests and responds to them. But it's not for us to question the purposes and actions of his sovereign will. Instead we're to submit to and accept whatever he has for us. And as we respond to his answers to our prayers, we must continue to acknowledge our dependence on him through more prayer. As we cycle through our prayers and his answers in this way, our dependency grows. No wonder those who regularly practice this spiritual discipline often speak of there being power in prayer. The more prayer, the more dependency; the more dependency, the more power. The source of power is not the prayer; it is the Holy Spirit, who uses prayer as a means of grace through which he provides the power.

Circumstances

A fourth instrument the Holy Spirit uses is the circumstances he allows or brings into our lives. Paul wrote:

> We know that for those who love God all things work together for good, for those who are called according to his purpose. For those whom he foreknew he also predestined to be conformed to the image of his Son, in order that he might be the firstborn among many brothers. (Romans 8:28–29)

Note that God causes *all* things—all circumstances, events, and the actions of other people, whether "good" or "bad" in our estimation—to work together for our ultimate good, which is conformity to the image of his Son. Our response should be to continually reflect on the various circumstances that come our way, especially the difficult ones, and seek to profit from them according to his will.

However, it's not only the difficult circumstances of life that should get our attention. We are also responsible to cultivate the habit of responding to the "good" circumstances by recognizing that they, too, are from his hand and part of Christ's purchased grace, which the Spirit of God distributes to us. In this way we learn to depend on the gracious, loving work of the Holy Spirit, as he in his infinite wisdom arranges and adapts all our circumstances to accomplish God's purposes for us. As we reflect on our lives during our daily communion with God, he often enables us to see our circumstances for what they really are—a means of grace.

Each of these instruments of the Holy Spirit is worthy of a more amplified discussion, and there are others we haven't covered. But our aim in this chapter has been to balance our earlier emphasis on dependence with an equally valid emphasis on our responsibility. We know how difficult it is to keep these parallel truths in proper relationship to one another. Our tendency is to stress one and neglect the other. For the two of us, we usually err on the side of overlooking our need for dependence. So we encourage one and all to learn the art of practicing *dependent responsibility*.

COMMUNION WITH GOD

What's the point of the Spirit using all of these means of grace in the life of the believer? All the means of grace are actually centered in one common purpose—communion with God. The word used most often in the Bible for this communion is *fellowship*. Paul wrote, "God is faithful, by whom you were called into the fellowship of his Son, Jesus Christ our Lord" (1 Corinthians 1:9). And John wrote, "That which we have seen and heard we proclaim also to you, so that you too may have fellowship with us; and indeed our fellowship is with the Father and with his Son Jesus Christ" (1 John 1:3).

This fellowship is both objective and subjective in nature. Objectively, it's an unbreakable union with Christ. In this sense, every believer has fellowship with him at all times. This objective aspect is undoubtedly what Paul was referring to in 1 Corinthians 1:9. In addition, God intends for us to *experience* and *enjoy* this fellowship with him as we consciously spend time in his presence. This subjective aspect of fellowship is likely what John had in mind in 1 John 1:3. And this is the type of fellowship we refer to as *communion*. Communion is the experience of our union.

One illustration of this is the marriage relationship. When we marry someone, there's an objective aspect to it—a legal union is formed the moment we say "I do." That's our status, even when we're apart or feel emotionally distant. But subjectively, we can experience a close and warm relationship as we spend time enjoying one another.

Desire for communion with God is vividly described in the Psalms. "O God, you are my God; earnestly I seek you; my soul thirsts for you; my flesh faints for you, as in a dry and weary land where there is no water" (Psalm 63:1). And: "As a deer pants for flowing streams, so pants my soul for you, O God. My soul thirsts for God, for the living God. When shall I come and appear before God?" (Psalm 42:1–2).

This concept of communion may be easy enough to

see and understand intellectually, but we need more than intellectual assent and understanding; we need *application*. We need this truth to become our daily practice *and* our heart's desire. For that to happen, we are dependent on the enabling power of the Holy Spirit as we work diligently at the spiritual disciplines. It is with this in mind that we offer the next chapter.

CHAPTER EIGHT

THE HELP OF THE DIVINE ENCOURAGER

By the power of the Holy Spirit you may abound in hope.
ROMANS 15:13

One of the most important aspects of the second book-end is the hope the Holy Spirit provides to believers. Every believer needs this divine encouragement because our opposition is relentless, and there are plenty of disappointments along the way. Sometimes we think we've turned the corner on a particular sin, only to discover a few days later that we've merely gone around the block and are dealing with it again. But there *is* hope in our battle with sin, and it lies in placing our dependence on the power of the Holy Spirit, our ever-present Helper (John 14:16–17).

The Holy Spirit often provides hope for the battle by pointing us back to the righteousness of Christ—the first bookend. Paul alluded to this when he wrote, "*Through the Spirit*, by faith, we ourselves eagerly wait for *the hope of righteousness*" (Galatians 5:5). There's nothing more encouraging for the battle-weary believer than to receive a fresh view of the righteousness of Christ. Strengthened by the gospel, we find renewed courage to lean hard on the second bookend while we actively participate in the process of transformation. This is yet another reason we never outgrow or move past the first bookend.

We're going to discuss four ways the Holy Spirit encourages us, and it's our prayer that they would become living realities in your heart as the Spirit encourages you to renew your dependence on the second bookend by remembering the first.

LIFE-CHANGING GRATITUDE FOR PURCHASED GRACE

Jesus said, "When the Helper comes . . . he will bear witness *about me*" (John 15:26). What does he have to relate to us about Jesus? He opens the eyes of our hearts to the gospel—the most encouraging news of all. He reminds us that Jesus said things such as "greater love has no one than this, that someone lay down his life for his friends" (John 15:13). We didn't deserve to be loved to the death; it's pure grace, the amazing and undeserved blessings of privilege and power purchased for us by Christ's obedient life and death. The Spirit's witness about the infinitely costly work paid for us by an infinitely valuable Person causes our hearts to see Christ in such a way that gratitude transforms us at the very core of our being. Paul explained it like this:

> For the love of Christ controls us, because we have con-
> cluded this: that one has died for all, therefore all have died;
> and he died for all, that those who live might no longer live
> for themselves but for him who for their sake died and was
> raised. (2 Corinthians 5:14–15)

The love Paul refers to here is not our love for Christ. If it were, he would have said "love *for* Christ controls us." Instead he says "love *of* Christ," which clearly refers to his love for us, a love forever proven at the cross. As our experience of Christ's love grips us more deeply, our gratitude for the grace he purchased gradually overcomes the vise-grip of our self-centeredness, and we "no longer live for ourselves." This illumination into Christ's great love is born in us only through the work of the Spirit.

John echoed this principle when he wrote, "In this the love of God was made manifest among us, that God sent his only Son into the world, so that we might live through him. In this is love, *not that we have loved God but that he loved us* and sent his Son to be the propitiation[1] for our sins." A few verses later John added, "We love because he first loved us" (1 John 4:9–10, 19). Our gratitude for the love that provided the first bookend encourages us to depend on the second for strength to obey the commandments, including the greatest ones—to love God with all our heart, soul, mind, and strength, and to love our neighbor as ourselves.

A great way to apply this is exemplified by the pastor friend we quoted earlier who was learning to shift his dependence away from functional saviors. He refuses to leave home in the morning until a deep awareness of God's love for him in the gospel is renewed. He works at this each morning through the spiritual disciplines of Bible meditation and prayer, but he's dependent on the Holy Spirit all the while. Since he started this habit, he is often encouraged by grace and strengthened for the daily battle against his functional saviors. And by sharing this aspect of his life with others, many who were once spiritually paralyzed and numb in his church have been awakened to the gospel and are being transformed as well.

By revisiting the gospel daily, we too can keep a deep sense of gratitude "bubbling up" like a steady spring in our lives as the Holy Spirit illuminates Christ's great love for us each day. Such gratitude will keep us encouraged even in times when we don't feel we're making any progress.

THE EXPULSIVE POWER OF A NEW AFFECTION

For many years, the two of us thought that the mind was the best weapon against the sins of the heart. We attempted to use our knowledge of "what I *should* do" to fight our sinful desire of "what I *want* to do." We assumed that if the argument of our mind prevailed, we would do the right thing. Diagram 8.1 illustrates our old approach to battling sin.

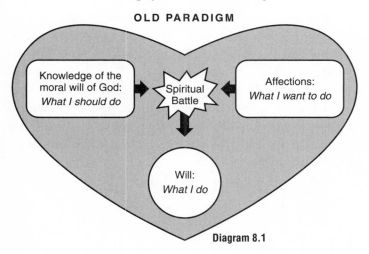

OLD PARADIGM

Knowledge of the moral will of God: *What I should do*

Spiritual Battle

Affections: *What I want to do*

Will: *What I do*

Diagram 8.1

However, this approach resulted in very limited success.

A sermon by the nineteenth-century Scottish minister Thomas Chalmers helped us immensely. Called "The Expulsive Power of a New Affection,"[2] the title alone speaks volumes. Here's an excerpt from Chalmers's sermon that we've updated into modern language:

> The best way to disengage an impure desire is to engage a pure one; the best way to expel the love of what is evil is to embrace the love of what is good instead. To be specific, we must replace the object of our sinful affection with an infinitely more worthy one—God himself. In this way we do not move from a full heart into a vacuum. Instead we move from a full heart to a heart bursting with fullness. And the expulsive power of our new affection weakens and even destroys the power of sin in our hearts.

Chalmers's point is that we must battle desire with desire. Whichever desire is the strongest will always determine the outcome. Paul also wrote about this battle against sin in terms of two competing desires: "The desires of the flesh are against the Spirit, and the desires of the Spirit are against the flesh, for these are opposed to each other, to keep you from doing the things you want to do" (Galatians 5:17). Diagram 8.2 is the diagram we now use to more accurately illustrate the battle.

NEW PARADIGM

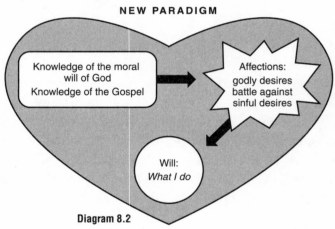

Knowledge of the moral will of God
Knowledge of the Gospel

Affections:
godly desires
battle against
sinful desires

Will:
What I do

Diagram 8.2

Ultimately, our godly desires must overcome our sinful desires if we're to obey God. So to win the battle against sin, we must strengthen and encourage our godly desires. How? By simultaneously growing in our awareness of: (1) our sin—our knowledge of the moral will of God and how far short we fall daily; and (2) God's love—the grace and blessings purchased by Christ in the gospel.

Though we work hard at this, we ultimately need the Divine Encourager to make it happen. Jesus said that when the Helper comes, "he will convict the world concerning sin and righteousness" (John 16:8). As the Spirit testifies to our sin and to the righteousness Christ graciously provides in the first bookend, our hearts are gripped by the immensity of the gap between what we deserve and the blessings purchased by Christ's obedient death. As we become increasingly desperate for the gospel, our sinful desires are expelled from our heart because they're replaced with a new desire for the God who demonstrated "his love for us in that while we were still sinners, Christ died for us" (Romans 5:8). As a simple yet practical application of this understanding, we might preach the following one-sentence sermon to ourselves every day: "Because he loves me so much, I love him more than _____."

As we see how incomparably desirable God is, he becomes our superior satisfaction, our all-surpassing treasure (Matthew 13:44). Our appetite for sin grows weak by comparison, and we expel it because there's not room enough in our heart for both. Our affection—our love for God—is then expressed in personal obedience and deepened relationship with the Father and the Son through the Holy Spirit. As Jesus said, "Whoever has my commandments and keeps them, he it is who loves me. And he who loves me will be loved by my Father, and I will love him and manifest myself to him. . . . And we will come to him and make our home with him" (John 14:21, 23).

ENJOYING THE RELATIONSHIP

The Westminster Confession of Faith provides a succinct and extraordinary statement of our purpose in life: "The chief end of man is to glorify God and enjoy him forever." We hear a lot about what it means to glorify God, but little is taught about what it means to really enjoy him. As believers, we're meant to enjoy God in the here and now as well as in heaven. And we enjoy him when we experience him in an active and intimate relationship of communion.

The gospel is the news that we can have such a relationship. Christ came with a particular goal in mind: "Christ also suffered once for sins, the righteous for the unrighteous, *that he might bring us to God*" (1 Peter 3:18). In Christ, the sinless sin bearer, God qualified believing sinners to enter into a favorable, intimate, and enjoyable relationship with him. Remarkably, as adopted members of the family of God we can literally *bask* in the love shared between the members of the Trinity. As we'll demonstrate, this is not an overstatement or a mere metaphor.

The entire seventeenth chapter of the Gospel of John records the prayer Jesus prayed before he entered the garden of Gethsemane on the night before his death. It's one of the most remarkable portions in all of Scripture; it provides us with an amazing glimpse behind the curtain into the inner workings of the Trinity. Jesus not only prayed for his disciples, he also prayed for *us* (John 17:20). In a single, monumental sentence, Jesus tells the Father two things that take our breath away:

> *The glory that you have given me I have given to them*, that they
> may be one even as we are one, I in them and you in me, that
> they may become perfectly one, so that the world may know
> that *you . . . loved them even as you loved me.* (John 17:22–23)

This is an incredible statement! Because of our union with Christ, the Father loves us the same way he loves the Son,[3] and the glory the Father has given to the Son is in turn given to us by the Son. Therefore, the glorifying love that exists within the Trinity is shed upon us and shared by us in such a way that we are capable of experiencing communion with the triune God that is enjoyable beyond measure.

To use a Puritan phrase, we have "exquisite moments"[4] when we experience this. Sometimes we can even bask in intimate, glorious love for quite a while. It's the worship-driven life. It's heaven on earth. Yet before long we recognize that our sin clouds our experience of it once again.

Meanwhile, the Holy Spirit uses our growing appetite for enjoying our relationship with God as a powerful encouragement in our battle against sin. He causes us to pause when we consider turning our backs on God in order to enjoy sin's fleeting pleasures instead. When we're tempted, he reminds us of the second bookend, and we are motivated to fall down in desperate dependence, and to beg, "Enable me to fight this sin so I might abide in relationship with you." When we enjoy God more than sin, we give him an even deeper level of glorifying love, a level he alone deserves.

The Holy Spirit truly is the Divine Encourager. Directly before Jesus began his prayer, he said this about the Spirit: "He will glorify me, for he will take what is mine and declare it to you" (John 16:14). The Spirit declares what is Christ's—*glory*! The blazing center of his glory is seen at the cross where he accomplished what no one else could do by opening our access into a relationship so satisfying, so intimate, and so desirable that it provides a continuous offer we cannot refuse: a relationship with God that is so enjoyable it makes other pleasures appear as they really are—small by comparison. And that is why, for the two of us, the greatest source of encouragement in our battle against sin is often our Spirit-driven desire to experience this enjoyment. You can't enjoy sin and God at the same time.

THE PROMISES OF GOD

Another powerful way the Holy Spirit encourages us to lean our books on the second bookend is to point us to truth. Jesus told the disciples, "When the Spirit of truth comes, he will guide you into all the truth" (John 16:13). What is this truth? At one point in his ministry Jesus said, "I . . . am the truth" (John 14:6); soon afterward he said *God's Word* was truth (John 17:17). The Spirit points us both to Jesus, our source of our righteousness for justification, and to the truth of God's written Word, the Bible, to help us in our battle with sin and to grow in Christlikeness.

In his role as our Encourager, the Spirit frequently leads us to specific promises of God. For the most part, when the Spirit guides us to God's promises, they're for use in our immediate or near future. They provide us with assurance that when we take a step of faith, as our weight shifts forward and our foot descends, God's grace and truth will arrive in time to support our foot as it lands. The promises equip us in the moment-by-moment heat of our battles against sin. Even when we don't experience the immediate fulfillment of the promise, we can always be certain he'll fulfill his promise in his own way and in his own perfect timing.

Living by faith in the future grace[5] promised in the Bible definitely has a purifying power. As Paul said, "Since we have these promises, beloved, let us cleanse ourselves from every defilement of body and spirit, bringing holiness to completion in the fear of God" (2 Corinthians 7:1). Peter put it like this:

> He has granted to us his precious and very great promises, so that *through them* you may become partakers of the divine nature, having escaped from the corruption that is in the world because of sinful desire. (2 Peter 1:4)

Though the Spirit often gives us momentary strength through the promises of God, the Spirit also directs us to promises to equip us for events that may not take place right away. When this occurs, we need to collect these promises so we can have easy access to them in a future battle. Journaling is a good way to do this. But we believe the best method may very well be Scripture memorization. The psalmist would agree: "I have stored up your word in my heart, that I might not sin against you" (Psalm 119:11).

Some of the most motivating promises of God are the ones designed to point us toward heaven and our eternal life with God. Jesus said, "The Spirit of truth . . . will declare to you the things that are to come" (John 16:13). Paul elaborated on this truth: "As it is written, 'What no eye has seen, nor ear heard, nor the heart of man imagined, what God has prepared for those who love him'— these things God has revealed to us through the Spirit. For the Spirit searches everything, even the depths of God" (1 Corinthians 2:9–10).

Ultimately these promises motivate greater dependence on the second bookend as we face our own death or the death of a loved one. They give us hope and confidence in God, the sovereign provider and sustainer of life—the very God who created our lives and will preserve our lives to eternity and cause us to have a peace that passes understanding, even in death, because we hold fast to his promises (Colossians 3:1–4).

The promises of eternal life stored up in our heart through the work of the Holy Spirit empower us to walk through the most difficult of life's trials and tragedies *and* glorify God in the process. The promises become the anchor of our soul (Hebrews 6:19) as we hold to the Rock of our Salvation.

Whether we live or die, the Spirit sustains us through the promises of God (Philippians 1:19–21). Along these lines, John wrote:

> Beloved, we are God's children now, and what we will be
> has not yet appeared; but we know that when he appears
> we shall be like him, because we shall see him as he is. (1
> John 3:2)

This verse stretches our imaginations to the limit. What will it be like to see God as he is? And to be like him? It thrills our hearts and minds and fills us with hope. But John added a caveat for the here-and-now: "And everyone who thus hopes in him purifies himself as he is pure" (verse 3). These same promises also provide a powerful purifying and sanctifying effect.

Isn't it amazing to ponder all the ways the Holy Spirit works to provide us with divine encouragement? And because he is God, we will never lack the grace we need for every moment.

Meanwhile, there is another gospel enemy we have yet to discuss, and it may be the most insidious one of all.

CHAPTER NINE

GOSPEL ENEMY #3: SELF-RELIANCE

*Therefore let anyone who thinks that he stands
take heed lest he fall.*

1 CORINTHIANS 10:12

Most of us would agree that Gospel Enemy #1 (self-righteousness) is repulsive, and that Gospel Enemy #2 (persistent guilt) is miserable, pitiful, and even pathetic. But it's different with Gospel Enemy #3, self-reliance. This one seems, well, desirable. The cousins of self-reliance also seem attractive: self-confidence, self-sufficiency, and our contemporary culture's favorite, self-esteem. You may be wondering what could possibly be wrong with these things. How could they be an enemy to the gospel?

Most of us were brought up to see self-reliance and its cousins as positive qualities, not enemies. We start learning to be self-reliant at an early age. By adolescence we've been taught to value independence as one of the greatest virtues. We eventually become convinced that ideally we shouldn't rely on anything or anyone other than ourselves—that whatever strength we need may be found within ourselves if we dig deep enough. Parents, siblings, friends, teachers, coaches, and even many preachers declare and sometimes literally shout this message. And it's constantly reinforced by television shows, movies, advertising, novels, self-help books, magazines, lyrics, motivational seminars, and popular slogans like Nancy Reagan's "Just say no" to drugs. Messages like these permeate our culture at a conscious and, more often, unconscious level. With one accord they assure us we can accomplish anything if we'll just believe in ourselves and try hard enough.

But the biblical idea of looking outside ourselves for strength runs counter to this paradigm. It seems foreign to us. And even if we manage to gain an understanding of this biblical truth, we flounder as we try to apply it. Why? We've been force-fed the doctrine of self-reliance for so long that it's embedded into the very fabric of our souls. So we should not be surprised to discover we're self-reliant toward God, as well.

Self-reliance toward God is a dependence on our own power, not the power of the Holy Spirit. Self-reliance is to the second bookend what self-righteousness is to the first. Self-righteousness is the opposite of dependence on Christ's righteousness for justification. Self-reliance is the opposite of dependence on the Holy Spirit's power for sanctification. Just as by nature we assume we earn our salvation by our good works, so by nature we assume we grow spiritually by our own effort and willpower.

What's wrong with this kind of self-reliance? Everything.

First of all, it doesn't work. The Christian life is a spiritual life lived in a spiritual world. Our human strength, be it physical power or willpower, is inadequate. We need divine strength that comes from a divine source—the Spirit of God. When we attempt to live the Christian life in our own strength, we head in the direction of legalism, pride, frustration, or ungodly living. It can even lead to a shipwrecked faith. When we nullify the grace of God provided in the second bookend, it's just a matter of time before we nullify it in the first bookend as well. That's why self-reliance is a gospel enemy.

Jesus told the disciples, "Apart from me you can do nothing" (John 15:5). Really? *Nothing*? The fact is that we're dependent on God for every single breath and heartbeat. When he says *stop*, our heart ceases. James affirmed this:

> Come now, you who say, "Today or tomorrow we will go into such and such a town and spend a year there and trade and make a profit"—yet you do not know what tomorrow will bring. What is your life? For you are a mist that appears for a little time and then vanishes. Instead you ought to say, "If the Lord wills, we will live and do this or that." As it is, you boast in your arrogance. All such boasting is evil. (James 4:13–16)

Self-reliance, like self-righteousness and persistent guilt, is sin. These gospel enemies entice us to redirect our dependencies to objects of faith outside the bookends, such as our strength, our righteousness, or our functional saviors. All such misdirected faith is cosmic treason. Paul put it like this: "The faith that you have, keep between yourself and God. . . . Whatever does not proceed from faith is sin" (Romans 14:22–23). Furthermore, if we perceive we've succeeded on our own, in our arrogance we'll boast, take the credit, and steal the glory. That, too, is sin.

Are we saying we shouldn't be self-reliant about *anything*? Yes, that's exactly what we're saying. Because in reality, self-reliance is an illusion, a lie. There's no such thing as self-made people who have pulled themselves up by their own bootstraps. If some appear to have succeeded by sheer determination and tenacious effort, we should ask, "If they have the ability to see and think and move a finger, where did *that* come from? As Paul put it, "What do you have that you did not receive?" (1 Corinthians 4:7).

We need to admit that self-reliance is a subtle and insidious enemy of our souls. But most of the time we don't even realize we're disregarding the second bookend. With one breath we express awareness that we're dependent on God for everything, and with the next breath we express self-reliance.

Earlier we described how all believers tend to vacillate between Gospel Enemies #1 and #2. Now here's another sobering statement: All believers are inclined to fall prey to Gospel Enemy #3 every day. How many times in the past twenty-four hours have we done *anything* with conscious dependence on the power of the Holy Spirit? How many of our job issues, family matters, leisure pursuits, daily routines, or even our spiritual disciplines have we conducted with an attitude of self-reliance, not God-reliance? Even as this chapter is being written, we struggle as authors to rely on God's strength and not merely our own natural ability and self-effort.

After the Last Supper, on the way to the Mount of Olives Jesus revealed to the disciples, "You will all fall away because of me this night. For it is written, 'I will strike the shepherd, and the sheep of the flock will be scattered.'" Peter responded, "Though they all fall away because of you, I will never fall away." Jesus countered with the truth that before the rooster crowed, Peter would deny him three times, to which Peter confidently retorted, "Even if I must die with you, I will not deny you!" (Matthew 26:31–35).

What was the object of Peter's dependence? It was his willpower. "*I will* never fall away; *I will* not deny you." He assumed he had the strength to stand where others would fall. After all, he was at the Mount of Transfiguration with Jesus, Moses, and Elijah (Luke 9:28–36). And he was the only disciple to walk on water (Matthew 14:23–33). But as Jesus was being spit on and slapped and mocked, Peter's strength collapsed. After he denied Jesus with three outbursts of swearing and cursing, "The Lord turned and looked at Peter. And Peter remembered . . . and he went out and wept bitterly" (Luke 22:54–62).

It was a most shameful experience for Peter. But aren't we just as guilty of relying on our own strength in order to remain faithful to Jesus? Since our strength is imperfect and the Holy Spirit's strength is flawless, every time we deny Jesus in the slightest way, it indicates we're depending on our own power, not his. We're not much different from Peter when we express frustration with the person who cuts us off on the freeway and then remember our sign-of-the-fish bumper sticker. We're not that much different from Peter when we join in the laughter when coworkers enjoy a less than edifying joke before remembering the Bible sitting out on our desk. Unfortunately, we can all think of countless examples in our day-to-day lives when we fail to draw on the power of the Spirit in order to remain faithful to Christ.

The apostle Paul was a very competent person, and he made one of the most frequently quoted "can-do" statements in history. Taken out of context, it sounds all-inclusive: "I *can do* all things . . . " But Paul put a God-sized qualifier on it: ". . . through him who strengthens me" (Philippians 4:13). Think of the enormous gulf between Paul's can-do statement and the Nike slogan, *Just do it*.

Let us introduce you to our friend Brian. In his fifties, he remains very athletic. He has everything Nike: shoes, wristbands, even a golf bag. His motto is *Just try harder*. It seemed to work well for him; he succeeded in college, career, and sports. His Christian journey began as a teenager. In high school he excelled in the spiritual disciplines, especially Scripture memorization. As he left home for college, his faith was vibrant and growing. Yet when we met him thirty years later, he was spiritually bankrupt and completely devastated. What happened?

In college, Brian's motivation for applying himself to

the spiritual disciplines gradually shifted from grateful delight in God to a subtle sense that God would reward him for performing these duties. Brian's other motto was *No pain, no gain.* He fully expected to gain as a result of enduring the pain of getting up early and exercising his mind over Scripture and prayer. Legalism always begins like that—with a trace of belief that we earn God's approval and blessings by our performance. As the seeds of self-reliance developed into a full-blown belief system, Brian's unwritten list of dos and don'ts began to loom larger. And when legalism blooms, its fruit is a prevailing and accelerating pressure to perform.

As long as Brian dug deeper, he continued to succeed. He worked harder and harder to keep up with Bible study, prayer lists, and Scripture memorization. He also labored over his grades. When he struggled against sin, he turned to his mottos, his white-knuckled willpower, and his above-average intestinal fortitude. But the pressure was beginning to show through the cracks. One day his campus ministry leader shared this passage on self-sufficiency:

> Not that we are sufficient in ourselves to claim anything as coming from us, but our sufficiency is from God, who has made us competent to be ministers of a new covenant, not of the letter but of the Spirit. For the letter kills, but the Spirit gives life. (2 Corinthians 3:5–6)

The words stuck in Brian's throat—he recognized the stark contradiction between this and his own approach to spirituality. But unfortunately, the leader failed to help him recognize and apply the truth about the righteousness of Christ (the first bookend) and the Spirit who gives life (the second bookend). Within a few weeks, Brian reverted to self-reliant legalism. Inwardly Brian pointed to his many successes as evidence that God was blessing him because he was measuring up. But before long, instead of the *atta-boys* he was accustomed to, his feedback from others included words like *arrogance* and *conceited*.

When we're doing well at meeting the self-imposed demands of our self-reliant approach to God and life, it inevitably leads to pride. It makes sense, doesn't it? If I do the work, I get the credit, not God. And from our perspective, it seems that others are merely jealous of our competence.

Brian eventually snapped under the pressure to perform. It was a secret, persistent sin that eventually defeated him. He couldn't beat that one. So in frustration, he gravitated away from the campus fellowship and concentrated on his studies, his tennis, and his girlfriend. Brian graduated, got a high-paying job, got married, and had two kids. Though he continued to go to church, he was just going through the motions. He settled into the mediocrity of what we call a cruise-control Christian—one who goes to church and avoids scandalous sins but has no genuine and heartfelt relationship with God. By his mid-thirties, he quit going to church. "I was too busy with my career," he said. At age forty he had a moral meltdown. "I threw out the baby with the bathwater," he told us sadly. When we met him eight years later, Brian was racked by persistent guilt.

Thankfully, he was also desperate for the gospel and ready to receive God's grace by embracing the bookends.

Isn't it ironic that the more God-given natural abilities we have, the more prone we are to rely on them rather than on God? But while some people are more gifted than others, all of us are endowed with various kinds of talents and abilities. And we have a tendency to lean on them, no matter how meager they are. Because Gospel Enemy #3 is an enemy we all share all the time—young or old, rich or poor—we don't need to ask ourselves a list of probing questions to see if we're under attack from this enemy. Even mature believers who are wheelchair bound have reported struggling with self-reliance.[1]

One way the Spirit of God helps free us from self-reliance is by revealing our sinfulness while simultaneously leading us back to the bookends. John Newton skillfully described this in his letters. We've updated a few of his sentences here into modern language:[2]

- When we acknowledge that our hearts are deceitful and that our lives are full of weakness, stubbornness, ingratitude, and foolishness, we discover to our surprise that in Christ, none of this can separate us from the love of God. In those moments Jesus becomes more precious to us.
- As the Spirit reveals the truth about our depravity, we're astonished to see that when we wandered from him, he retrieved us; when we fell, he lifted us; when we were wounded, he healed us; and when we fainted for lack of strength, he revived us.
- The very best views we've had of his goodness, faithfulness, mercy, and grace have come in the context of a fresh

revelation of our vileness. If we hadn't known so much of
ourselves, we wouldn't have known so much of him.

- As the truth about our remaining sinfulness grips us, we
experience pain. But this is actually a merciful blessing; by
it, the Spirit weakens our self-reliance. He then points us
to two bigger truths: the cross and his power. The result:
we treasure the gospel more highly than we did before we
experienced the pain.

Sometimes the actions of the Holy Spirit in freeing us
from self-reliance are not directly related to our sin. Such
is the case with Paul's "thorn in the flesh" (2 Corinthians
12:7–8). No one knows exactly what this was, but it must
have been painful either physically or emotionally. Paul
begged the Lord three times to take it away. But God didn't
remove the thorn. He did something far better. He provided Paul with a monumental promise: "My grace is sufficient for you, for my power is made perfect in weakness"
(2 Corinthians 12:9).

Paul's incredible response was to embrace the divine
source of strength available from the second bookend.
There's no other explanation for how he could live the radical Christian life, demonstrated by what he writes next:

Therefore I will boast all the more gladly of my weaknesses,
so that the power of Christ may rest upon me. For the sake
of Christ, then, I am content with weaknesses, insults, hard-
ships, persecutions, and calamities. For when I am weak,
then I am strong. (2 Corinthians 12:9–10)

In this episode of Paul's life, God-reliance took the

place of self-reliance. For the moment, Gospel Enemy #3 was crushed to powder, and life-changing power for sacrificial service was released. This should inspire us all, for we have the same God as Paul did.

But in spite of this resounding victory, Paul continued to do battle with Gospel Enemy #3 until the very end (Philippians 3:12–14). The same is true with us. Since our tendency to rely on ourselves is so pervasive, what are we to do? If it seems hopeless, rest assured it is not. In the next chapter we'll discuss specific strategies for the battle.

CHAPTER TEN

LEANING ON THE SECOND BOOKEND

We look not to the things that are seen but to the things
that are unseen. For the things that are seen are transient,
but the things that are unseen are eternal.

2 CORINTHIANS 4:18

God has provided the power of the Holy Spirit for those who are covered by the righteousness of Christ. And just like the first bookend, the second is infinitely solid and weighty. However, we've seen that we're constantly inclined to disregard the second bookend and lean our books on ourselves instead—our natural abilities, our strength, our resources. Consequently, our lives become a series of reality checks where we're reminded again and again that our self-reliance is only an illusion; we just don't have what it takes to support the weight of our own books. We must shift our dependence, or our books will fall.

In this chapter we offer three focal points for shifting our dependence to the second bookend. Like the first set of focal points we offered for shifting our dependence to the first bookend, these also require *seeing* something. This time we're to see "the immeasurable greatness of his power toward us who believe, according to the working of his great might" (Ephesians 1:18–19). We're to see this with the eyes of our hearts in such a way that it touches our emotions, motivations, and decision-making. It's a seeing so deep, it shifts our dependence away from our own strength and onto the strength of the Spirit of God.

FOCAL POINT #1:
OUR DESPERATE WEAKNESS

Can you think of anything weaker than the lowly earthworm? In the beak of its enemy, the bird, it has neither offensive nor defensive power. It's not only desperately weak but also utterly helpless.

Though you may see no resemblance between you and a worm, and you may even be offended by the comparison, that's how God sees us. He told his chosen people, "Fear not, you worm Jacob, you men of Israel! I am the one who helps you, declares the LORD; your Redeemer is the Holy One of Israel" (Isaiah 41:14).

Before you get insulted, realize that God isn't literally calling us worms. It's a metaphor mercifully designed to reveal something we need to see about ourselves. Apart from receiving God's enabling power, we're as helpless as worms. And until we see this, we'll never be free from the stronghold of self-reliance. But once we shift our dependence to the second bookend, amazing things can happen. In the next two verses, God continues through Isaiah:

> Behold, I make of you a threshing sledge, new, sharp, and having teeth; you shall thresh the mountains and crush them, and you shall make the hills like chaff; you shall winnow them, and the wind shall carry them away, and the tempest shall scatter them. And you shall rejoice in the LORD; in the Holy One of Israel you shall glory. (Isaiah 41:15–16)

No longer helpless worms, the enabling help of our holy Redeemer transforms us into useful, powerful tools— threshing sledges that crush mountains. The passage concludes with a thought-provoking idea: we get the joy, and God gets the glory.

The psalmist Asaph saw his share of bad days. Take, for example, the one he referred to in Psalm 73 where he wrote, "When my soul was embittered, when I was pricked in heart, I was brutish and ignorant; I was like a beast toward you" (verses 21–22). The Hebrew word for beast indicates a dumb, four-legged animal, like a cow. Not exactly an image of empowerment. He thought his body and his heart—his physical strength and willpower—might fail at any minute. But through these experiences, his dependence shifted and he exclaimed, "God is the strength of my heart and my portion forever" (verse 26).

Likewise for us, seeing ourselves as weak and helpless is a necessary step in shifting our dependence from our strength to his. We must stop relying on our own power before we're able to receive power from the Holy Spirit.

FOCAL POINT #2:
THE RELIABLE POWER OF THE
HOLY SPIRIT

As we once again ponder Paul's amazing statement in 2 Corinthians 3:18 about the process of our transformation into Christlikeness, note that this, too, involved seeing:

> And we all, with unveiled face, beholding the glory of the Lord, are being transformed into the same image from one degree of glory to another. For this comes from the Lord who is the Spirit.

Remarkably, as we see the glory of the Lord, we become like him. The theological term for this process is *progressive sanctification*. It starts at the point in time we are justified by trusting Christ, and it ends at the moment we depart from our physical body. And the power source for this gradual-but-radical transformation is "the Lord who is the Spirit." Progressive sanctification is an all-inclusive process. It encompasses all our "books"—both spiritual and temporal. Paul showed this when he wrote:

> Now may the God of peace himself sanctify you completely, and may your whole spirit and soul and body be kept blameless at the coming of our Lord Jesus Christ. (1 Thessalonians 5:23)

When we combine the two verses above, we conclude that our sanctification is a comprehensive, God-centered process mediated by the power of the Holy

Spirit, an infinite source of power. That sounds reliable enough, so we respond by shifting our dependence. And when we do, we have great expectations. But what happens next? Sometimes he "comes through" for us. But sometimes he doesn't, or so it seems. What's going on when we cast our dependence fully on God and he seems so unresponsive?

Here we must be reminded that as we depend on the power of the Holy Spirit, he transforms us according to *his* plan and timetable—which are rarely if ever in perfect conformity with our own. The reason he withholds empowerment from us is not that he lacks power or the ability to transmit power to us. It's because in his infinite wisdom, sovereignty, mercy, and love, he empowers only what is best for us.

Therefore, leaning our books on the second bookend doesn't necessarily mean things will go our way. It doesn't mean things will go smoothly or that we'll no longer be tempted. In Hebrews 11, faith is exemplified by great exploits performed by God's strength as his people trusted fully in him. Enemies both physical and spiritual were laid waste by the work of God through his saints. But then we read that the outcome wasn't always so wonderful, at least from a temporal perspective: some with equal faith and trust were sawn in two or forced to live in utter destitution, with nothing left but God. They must surely have been tempted to feel God had deserted them.

But rest assured we can rely on the power of the Holy Spirit to actively accomplish all of his divine intentions.

The worm Jacob might pray, "I depend on your help to make me an eagle so I can devour my enemy, the robin." But the Lord makes Jacob a threshing sledge instead. Power was delivered so that, according to God's plan, mountains could be crushed, not mere birds.

Think of it this way: we wage war in the power of another. It's a spiritual war, and the power is that of the Spirit of Almighty God. Paul wrote, "For though we walk in the flesh, we are not waging war according to the flesh. For the weapons of our warfare are not of the flesh but have *divine power* to destroy strongholds" (2 Corinthians 10:3–4). In every war there are setbacks and casualties; this one's no exception. But in the process, the Spirit of God continuously, proactively, and progressively conforms us to Christlikeness. That's definite. We can rely on it. He will accomplish it. Paul put it this way: "I am sure of this, that he who began a good work in you will bring it to completion at the day of Jesus Christ" (Philippians 1:6).

FOCAL POINT #3:
REJECTION OF SELF-RELIANCE

If you take even a cursory overview of your life with an eye to self-reliance, we expect you'll quickly detect it. If you don't, simply place your last twenty-four hours under the light of the following questions:

- How many times was I consciously aware of relying on the power of the Holy Spirit, instead of on myself?
- How many times did I acknowledge God's sovereign hand

and power sustaining my every endeavor—voluntary or involuntary, conscious or unconscious?

But *seeing* our self-reliance is the easy part; the challenge is *rejecting* it. Self-reliance is like the poison ivy one of our neighbors had in his backyard. By the time Mickey, his wife, their two toddlers, and his mother-in-law developed unspeakable cases of itching and oozing, he decided he'd had enough. He called it The Enemy.

At first, Mickey attacked it with his John Deere garden tractor. He tried to mow and scrape it to death. It popped back up within a few days. Next, he decided to douse it with kerosene and light a match. Instantly, thirty feet of spectacular black smoke rolled off the backyard. Two weeks later The Enemy was back.

Then Mickey got desperate. He put on rubber gloves, severed every visible vine, and yanked off every last leaf. Come midnight, he actually thought he could hear the poison ivy laughing outside his bedroom window. Sure enough, it eventually came back with a vengeance—twice as bad as it was in the first place.

To kill poison ivy, or self-reliance, you have to get it by the roots. The tap-root of self-reliance is ultimately found in the statement, "I will be as God." Adam and Eve embraced it as the motive for the original sin (Genesis 3:5–6). Long before that, Lucifer (Satan) said essentially the same thing: "I will make myself like the Most High" (Isaiah 14:13–14). This constitutes a declaration of independence from God. It's cosmic treason. But this attitude isn't limited to the likes of Adam, Eve, and Lucifer. It's at the root of the remaining sin nature in all of us.

All three gospel enemies spring forth from this common root. It's the essence of our self-reliance with its unspoken claim that *I* can do it myself. It's behind our ever-present bent toward self-righteousness, as well. If I'm my own god, *I* determine what's right and wrong, and *I* declare myself good enough. Even persistent guilt has its root in this statement, because it's a refusal to acknowledge and embrace the solution *God* has provided for our sin dilemma, as if to say, *I* will be my own judge.

Therefore, the focus of the battle with all three gospel enemies, and self-reliance in particular, should center on making a deliberate, repeated counter-declaration: "God is God, and I am not." And once we make that pronouncement each day, we must pray for opportunities and strength to apply it.

Mickey eventually used a herbicide designed to kill the roots of the poison ivy. But by the time The Enemy surrendered, there were sizable bare spots in the landscape. That's when Mickey got smart. He planted and cultivated two varieties of hardy perennials, daylilies and yellow irises. Three years later, the area that had once been a war zone was so thick with the new plants, there was no way poison ivy—or anything else—could take root there again.

Taking a lesson from both Mickey and the Bible, our daily war plan calls for us to kill self-reliance and replace it by planting and cultivating the daylilies of *humility* and the yellow irises of *godliness*.

C. J. Mahaney defines humility as "honestly assessing ourselves in light of God's holiness and our sinfulness."[1] We could easily substitute our word *seeing* for C. J.'s word *assessing*. John Stott described the best place to find the basis for such humility:

> Nothing in history or in the universe cuts us down to size like the cross. All of us have inflated views of ourselves . . . until we have visited a place called Calvary. It is there, at the foot of the cross that we shrink to our true size.[2]

Why is a fresh view of the cross needed in order to cultivate humility? When we see Jesus there bearing our sin, we also see exactly what we deserve from God for each sin we commit. Then and only then can we begin to honestly assess ourselves. The One whose flesh was nailed to the cross should have been us: "He was pierced through for our transgressions" (Isaiah 53:5, NASB). At the cross we see the holiness of God as well—his perfect justice served by unleashing his undiluted wrath against sin, as he punished and rejected the sin bearer in our place.

As we revisit the cross and linger there in meditation focused on its unending and unfathomable wonders, we cultivate a thick patch of the daylilies we call humility, and when this happens, there's no longer any room for the pride that leads to the desire to *be like God*.

Now for the irises. We define *godliness* as "the attitude of regarding God in everything all the time." We display this attitude when, no matter what we do, we "do all to the glory of God" (1 Corinthians 10:31). The godly person is a God-centered, God-glorifying, God-esteeming person. The opposite of godliness is ungodliness, the disregarding of God. All expressions of pride are rooted in ungodliness, because you must first disregard God before you can be prideful. So for us, the battle for godliness is the linchpin of our war plan.

How do we fight for godliness? It starts the same way we fight for humility—by seeing the cross as the over-arching message and meaning of life and the universe. From there we must discipline our minds to practice the presence of God, "and take every thought captive to obey Christ" (2 Corinthians 10:5).

Seeing and rejecting self-reliance and replacing it with humility and godliness always results in a shift of our dependence. But that shift isn't permanent; it must be continuously renewed daily at the foot of the cross.

A VIEW OF ALL THREE FOCAL POINTS

We can see all three focal points demonstrated in the life of Paul:

> When I came to you, brothers, [I] did not come proclaiming to you the testimony of God with lofty speech or wisdom. For I decided to know nothing among you except Jesus Christ and him crucified. (1 Corinthians 2:1–2)

Paul was a highly educated and intelligent man. He could easily reason with the best of them, including kings and emperors. In spite of this, he didn't rely on his natural abilities. He identified and rejected any tendency toward reliance on his substantial reservoir of wisdom. Instead, he pointed straight to the gospel, acknowledged his weakness, and regarded the power of the Holy Spirit as absolutely reliable. He said to the Corinthians:

> And I was with you in weakness and in fear and much trembling, and my speech and my message were not in plausible words of wisdom, but in *demonstration of the Spirit* and of *power*. (1 Corinthians 2:3–4)

Paul did this so that their "faith might not rest in the wisdom of men but in the power of God" (verse 5).

At this point in his letter, Paul takes them deeper, telling them of a "secret and hidden wisdom of God, which God decreed before the ages for our glory" (verse 7). Even a glimpse into this hidden wisdom would take our breath away. But what is it? And how do we get in on it?

Paul provided a hint by quoting the Old Testament: "No eye has seen, nor ear heard, nor the heart of man imagined, what God has prepared for those who love him" (verse 9). To understand the mystery, we must see the unseeable, hear the unhearable, and imagine the unimaginable. But how?

We get another clue when we look up the Old Testament passage Paul quoted here in 1 Corinthians 2:9: "From of old no one has heard or perceived by the ear, no eye has seen a God besides you, *who acts for those who wait for him*" (Isaiah 64:4). When we watch expectantly, we express dependence; we start to "see" the unseeable, then do the undo-able, as God acts.

Then Paul comes right out with it: we see the unsee-able through the Holy Spirit:

> These things God has revealed to us through the Spirit. . . .
> Now we have received . . . the Spirit who is from God, that
> we might understand the things freely given us by God. And
> we impart this in words not taught by human wisdom but
> taught by the Spirit, interpreting spiritual truths to those
> who are spiritual. (1 Corinthians 2:10–13)

Most believers realize Paul was Christ-centered and gospel-centered, but these verses show he was Spirit-centered as well. And his dependence was as riveted to the second bookend as it was to the first.

Keeping these three focal points in sight is a continual process for all of us. So, after preaching the gospel to our-selves early each morning, let's add this Daily Declaration of Dependence:

- I recognize my absolute lack of power and ability.
- I redirect my dependence to the supremely reliable power of the Holy Spirit.
- I reject my tendency to self-reliance: "You are God, and I am not."

With our dependence on both bookends renewed we proclaim to God, "We are your servants." We work hard in the strength he provides, not to earn merit but to glorify and enjoy him. We declare with Paul, "By the grace of

God I am what I am, and his grace toward me was not in vain. On the contrary, I worked harder than any of them, though it was not I, but the grace of God that is with me" (1 Corinthians 15:10). And we acknowledge "we have this treasure in jars of clay, to show that the surpassing power belongs to God and not to us" (2 Corinthians 4:7).

THE BOOKENDS
PERSONAL WORLDVIEW

Only in the LORD . . . are righteousness and strength.

ISAIAH 45:24

A worldview is an all-encompassing framework of ideas and beliefs through which an individual views and interacts with the world. It provides a system for both interpreting and applying knowledge. It functions like a grid through which we process our perception of reality. Or, to put it in other terms, our worldview is the way we view all of life, like a set of eyeglasses through which we see everything in the world.

Worldviews vary from person to person. Obviously the worldview we adopt has an enormous impact on our actions and decision-making processes.

Over the last few years, as the two of us have shared our personal issues and prayer requests, we have become aware of our failure to depend on either the righteousness of Christ or the power of the Holy Spirit. As a result, we have often found ourselves speaking to each other in terms of the first and second bookends.

Along the way it dawned on us that the bookends had become our worldview—all the activity of our hearts and minds could be framed and explained in "bookend" terminology.

We've noticed as well the abundant discussion in recent years about what constitutes a biblical worldview. We propose that the bookends provide one. It's not necessarily an all-inclusive one that covers apologetics, environmentalism, or global economics; most Christians just want to know, "How can I get through the day?" The bookends worldview is designed to address this level of need. Within the overall context of Scripture, the bookends offer a useful frame of reference that provides clarity and guidance for our day-to-day decision-making processes and actions. Thus we refer to the bookends as a *personal* worldview.

At any given time, all Christians are occupied in one or more of three arenas: either (1) we're battling sin; (2) we're actively sinning; or (3) we're in the aftermath of sin. In each of these three scenarios, the bookends worldview is applicable and helpful.

In the case of battling against sin, we must lean on the second bookend, the power of the Holy Spirit, to provide the strength we need to be obedient and not give in to temptation. The first bookend, the righteousness of Christ, also comes into play. As we look to the cross, we're motivated by overwhelming gratitude, a desire to abide in relationship, and a goal of returning love to him by our obedience.

In the case of actively sinning, we've failed to lean on either bookend. On one hand, we may have given in to self-righteousness or persistent guilt. On the other hand, we may have given in to self-reliance. Most likely it's a combination of both. But in all cases, having been tempted by the world, the devil, or our own flesh, it comes down to the fact that we haven't relied on the righteousness of Christ and the power of the Holy Spirit to receive the grace we need to avoid sinning.

When we're in the aftermath of sin, we must renew our dependence on the first bookend by preaching the gospel to ourselves. We must remember that Christ lived the life we should have lived, and died the death we should have died. His obedience unto death is all-sufficient for reconciling us to God. The second bookend comes into play here, as we rely on the Holy Spirit to reveal our sin, draw us to the cross, and enable our repentance and transformation.

One of us can recall a painful episode in which a family member exposed what most people would consider to be a small sin, if it was a sin at all. As can easily happen in families, the situation escalated. Needless to say, it was painful. Early the next morning, the Lord brought clarity through the bookends worldview: "Yes, it was a sin—you were disobedient. But yes, Jesus was obedient in your place, and you are accepted on his behalf. And by the power of the Spirit, you can repent, ask forgiveness, and change. And you can forgive those who have sinned against you." Both bookends stood firm, and through leaning on them, every need was met.

In addition to helping us process our battle with sin, the bookends worldview has also helped us in every kind of interpersonal relationship—marriage, parent and child, extended family, friends, authority figures, coworkers, and neighbors. We've found it to be applicable in every circumstance and circle of life, including career, ministry, stewardship, and service.

On top of all this, the bookends worldview has informed our decisions regarding our lifestyles, including the use of time, money, and all our resources. Most of all, understanding and applying this worldview has provided valuable insight and guidance when it comes to two often deceitful and difficult-to-discern areas of life: motivations and dependencies.

Why is the bookends worldview so useful and worthwhile? Because it provides a constant awareness of the two most fundamental realities that apply to our lives. It reminds us that we're 100 percent dependent on a source of righteousness and strength that resides outside ourselves, yet we remain 100 percent responsible for the placement of each of our books on the bookshelf of our lives. The bookends worldview provides grace and truth for every moment—exhortation, encouragement, correction, assurance, wisdom, guidance, enablement, and more. And because we never forget our absolute dependence, it's all to the glory of God, not us, even if we're involved in the working. Like Paul, the two of us recognize we have not yet arrived, but we press on and strain forward (Philippians 3:12–14) with the bookends as our guide.

The bookends are like the rod and staff of the Great Shepherd. With them he makes us lie down in green pastures, leads us beside still waters, and restores our souls. He also leads us in paths of righteousness for his name's sake. And though we walk through the valley of the shadow of death, we'll fear no evil, for the triune God is with us, comforting us with the rod and staff of the righteousness of Christ and the power of the Holy Spirit (Psalm 23:2–4).

For us, adopting the bookends as a worldview has been radically life-changing. We hope that you, too, will be blessed by applying this simple yet profound way of seeing and responding to your world. We humbly submit this worldview to you, not as another program or another self-help paradigm but as the application of biblical doctrine and transforming truth that stabilizes our faith and sanctifies our lives.

WHAT NEXT?

Once we've embraced the bookends worldview, what comes next?

We must ask ourselves, "Why are we here?" To answer that question, let's go back to the experience of the prophet Isaiah. When his anguish over his sinfulness was resolved by the seraph's announcement that his sins were atoned for, what was Isaiah's response? It was a grateful "Here am I! Send me" (Isaiah 6:8).

This reflects the ultimate goal of living between the bookends. The Christian life isn't merely about our personal justification and sanctification—keeping all our books in a row. It's also about fulfilling the Great Commission, going out into all the world and making disciples.

Instead of page after page and chapter after chapter of a storyline filled with self-righteousness, persistent guilt, and self-reliance, the pages and chapters of books that are stabilized by the bookends should tell an action-packed story of selfless serving, radical giving, and sacrificial living. The impact of being covered by the perfect righteousness of Christ and being enabled by the infinite power of the Holy Spirit should change everything. The result of living between the bookends should be a resounding, "Here am I, Lord; send me!"

We conclude with one of our favorite verses of Scripture, one that displays both bookends while expressing the reverential awe we share for the God who so graciously provided them:

> Now to him who is able *to keep you from stumbling* and *to present you blameless* before the presence of his glory with great joy, to the only God, our Savior, through Jesus Christ our Lord, be glory, majesty, dominion, and authority, before all time and now and forever. Amen. (Jude 24–25)

NOTES

INTRODUCTION

1. For example, see Matthew 23.

CHAPTER 1: THE RIGHTEOUSNESS OF CHRIST

1. These statements are validated in Romans 2:12–16.

2. Jerry Bridges and Bob Bevington, *The Great Exchange* (Wheaton, IL: Crossway, 2007) 41–45, 111–19, 159–64.

CHAPTER 3: GOSPEL ENEMY #1: SELF-RIGHTEOUSNESS

1. John Owen, *Communion with the Triune God*, ed. Kelly Kapic and Justin Taylor (Wheaton, IL: Crossway, 2007), 30.

CHAPTER 4: GOSPEL ENEMY #2: PERSISTENT GUILT

1. Jonathan Aitken, *John Newton: From Disgrace to Amazing Grace* (Wheaton, IL: Crossway, 2007), 374.

2. Original and abridged versions of Thomas Wilcox's essay "Honey out of the Rock" are widely available for no charge on the Internet.

3. John Owen, *Communion with the Triune God*, ed. Kelly Kapic and Justin Taylor (Wheaton, IL: Crossway, 2007), 162.

CHAPTER 5: LEANING ON THE FIRST BOOKEND

1. From our adaptation of Thomas Wilcox's "Honey out of the Rock."

2. Adapted from Ken Sande, *The Peacemaker* (Grand Rapids, MI: Baker, 2007), 105.

3. Joe Coffey, "How a Mega-Church Is Rediscovering the Gospel," *Themelios*, vol. 33, no. 1 (May 2008): 60–62.

CHAPTER 6: THE POWER OF THE HOLY SPIRIT

1. John Owen, *The Holy Spirit*, abridged R. J. K. Law (Carlisle, PA: Banner of Truth, 1998), 8, 19.

CHAPTER 8: THE HELP OF THE DIVINE ENCOURAGER

1. The word *propitiation* used here means "wrath bearer."
2. Original digital versions of Thomas Chalmers's sermon "The Expulsive Power of a New Affection" are widely available for no charge on the Internet.
3. It is also amazing to note that Jesus loves us the same way the Father loves him! See John 15:9.
4. "Exquisite moments" is an expression used by John Owen, Jonathan Edwards, and many other Puritan writers to describe moments of pleasure experienced in communion with God.
5. To fully unpack the meaning of this power-filled sentence, we highly recommend a book by John Piper, *Future Grace* (Sisters, OR: Multnomah, 1995).

CHAPTER 9: GOSPEL ENEMY #3: SELF-RELIANCE

1. We recommend the message by Joni Eareckson Tada delivered at the 2005 Desiring God National Conference. Free audio and video downloads are available at http://www.desiringGOD.org.
2. Adapted from *Letters of John Newton* (Carlisle, PA: Banner of Truth, 2000), 128, 133–34.

CHAPTER 10: LEANING ON THE SECOND BOOKEND

1. C. J. Mahaney, *Humility: True Greatness* (Sisters, OR: Multnomah, 2005), 22.
2. John Stott, *The Message of Galatians* (Downers Grove, IL: InterVarsity, 1968), 179.

SCRIPTURE INDEX